Weather eYe

ISSUE 14

The Coldest Place in Europe?

The "Highs and Lows" of Weather

The Summer of 2003

Weather eYe

"For everyone fascinated by the Weather."

A funnel cloud visible looking towards the South Downs near Eastbourne on Saturday afternoon 6th September 2003.
Picture by Chris Keating.
Later in the Autumn a tornado actually touched down in Bearstead, Kent, causing thousands of pounds worth of damage to bungalows. Curtains were sucked through the rubber of double glazed windows.

Front cover: *Sunset on the 19th November 2003 at Braintree, Essex. Picture by Philippe Hays.*

Back cover: *Autumn at Wescott near Dorking Surrey-5th November 2003 Picture by Ian Currie.*

What a year it has been weather-wise for sunshine, warmth and lack of rain. However 'be it dry or be it wet, Nature always pays its debt' is a good adage and the weather pendulum swung to unsettled in November.
Parts of Sussex had 9 days in a row without any sunshine. At my Coulsdon weather station I recorded 108 mm of rain in 10 days from the 17th November.
A big thank you to all readers for providing such an array of weather pictures and articles for issue 14. There was a good response to issue 13's competition. The winners are on page 18 and there is a new challenge in issue 14 that I hope many of you will try. Looking further ahead there is a major competition earmarked for issue 15.
Remember Weather eye makes a good Christmas or birthday present for friends or relations. If you would like an useful plastic wallet to store up to 10 issues we can provide them at a cost of 3 for £2.50 including postage. Send cheques to Frosted Earth or add it to the cost when you renew your subscription.
There is a slight increase of 25p to the subscription price for 3 issues. This is to cover increased printing costs so that three issues will now be £7 to include posting. Renewal for 6 issues though is a special rate of just £12.50.
May I wish everyone a very pleasant Christmas and healthy and happy New Year. The Weather I am sure will make 2004 a very interesting year ahead.
Ian Currie

For details on ***subscriptions*** *and updated* ***weather reports***
log on to ***www.frostedearth.com*** *or telephone* ***01737 554869***

Published by: Frosted Earth, 77 Rickman Hill, Coulsdon, Surrey CR5 3DT ***Printed by:*** Litho Techniques Ltd, 46-50 Godstone Road, Whyteleafe, Surrey CR3 0EA

BROGDALE WEATHER STATION IS ON A HIGH.

For a month or so Gravesend , Kent was proud of being the hottest place in the British Isles, with 38.1C on 10th August 2003. Or so they thought. In September news broke of a revaluation of those very high temperatures and a new record was established, 38.5C [101.3F] at Brogdale.

With remarkable coincidence I was due to give a talk near by that very afternoon, so I arrived early and went in search of Britain's hottest weather station. It is situated in the home of the National Fruit Collection at Brogdale, not far from where I was due to speak at Faversham, Kent. They kindly showed me over the now famous instrument enclosure *(see picture above)*. At the Centre's office I chatted to the lady in charge of the station, Mary Pennell and just before I arrived a large parcel had been delivered addressed from the Met. Office - a new instrument screen for them.

The time lag by the Met. Office in announcing this change came about because this station reports in on a monthly basis and instruments have to be scrutinized and verified if they record an outstanding reading.

Temperatures readings from Brogdale Weather station August 1st -15th 2003.

Courtesy of Mary Pennell.

DATE	MAX 'C	MIN 'C
August 1st	25.0	14.4
2nd	25.2	14.3
3rd	28.3	12.0
4th	27.1	12.6
5th	30.3	14.4
6th	35.9	15.9
7th	31.2	18.9
8th	28.0	14.9
9th	32.2	15.0
10th	38.5	15.5
11th	32.4	18.5
12th	30.2	17.5
13th	28.1	16.7
14th	22.4	15.7
15th	23.1	8.3

The site is surrounded by an immense variety of fruit trees, over 2300 kinds of apple and 550 types of pear alone.

There were several factors that helped to make Brogdale's recordbreaking heat. It is situated on the dip slope of the North Downs and the gentle south-south east winds on this day would make it the lee side where air would be subsiding and warming- a föhn affect. This part of Kent remained in sunshine whereas cloud developed over London and areas to the north of the Thames with thunderstorms in places. Also a short sea track across the narrowest part of the Channel from a very hot France meant little cooling, as it crossed open water.

Following on from my visit to Brogdale I enquired whether they could identify an old but very cherished apple tree in my garden. I gave them a specimen from the bountiful crop 2003 had produced.

So it was with great interest that I recently received news from Brogdale that it was indeed a very good variety not often seen these days- a Blenheim Orange. Excellent for eating and cooking; perfect with cheese and was used for making Apple Charlotte.

Apparently it was discovered growing against the boundary wall of Blenheim Park by a cobbler named Kempster in 1740. He moved it into his garden and thereupon it was visited by thousands of people who gazed upon its orange coloured fruit. Gardeners took scions for grafting and it became known as Kempster's Pippin but with the Duke of Marlborough's approval in 1804 was branded as the new Blenheim Orange.

I wondered how the tree survived 1740 for the winter was one of the most severe ever recorded and May that year was the coldest in our national record. Frosts were frequent and severe, yet that tree lived to tell the tale and its lineage is in my garden. However a botanist friend of mine said that apple trees need a least 60 cold days a year and in fact they may suffer under the warming trend we are now experiencing.

For details of events at Brogdale write to Brogdale Horticultural Trust Brogdale Road, Faversham Kent ME13 8XZ Tel 01795 535286

THE HIGHS AND LOWS

A quiet spell of weather in a winter 'high' at Virginia Water, Surrey. Picture by Mrs A Lewis.

It's probably true that more households possess a barometer than any other weather instrument. Not all that many people have a thermometer actually outside, where it could be called a weather instrument. Ironically, we are unable to sense air pressure, except the rapid changes that can occur in an aircraft or on the Underground, yet changes in air pressure are a fundamental part of weather, as we shall see.

The pressure of the atmosphere is just due to its weight above us. If the pressure falls there is less air up there. It's as simple as that, but it is not the pressure itself that causes the different types of weather in anticyclones and depressions (Highs and Lows respectively). Rather it is the processes (at all levels in the atmosphere) that bring about these pressure changes that also cause the weather associated with them.

But first let us look at the general atmospheric circulation, in which highs and lows can be regarded as huge eddies in a general current.

The polar regions are colder than the equator because they receive less sunlight, so a column of air above the arctic will be colder than one above the tropics. Since air contracts with cold this column will contain more of its air below a fixed height (typically 20,000-ft) than one over the tropics. The pressure at this height is therefore lower over the arctic. The wind, blowing anticlockwise round this Low, is therefore generally westerly in the upper atmosphere and it is this flow that brings us our succession of weather systems.

The general flow can become very distorted due to temperature differences between oceans and continents and when this happens (technically termed "blocking") a high-pressure area can stay around for weeks, giving us a cold winter spell or a summer heatwave. Now we must look at how the "eddies" in the westerly flow are formed and why they give us the weather they do. The westerly upper-air wind has a tendency to concentrate itself into relatively narrow bands of very high wind speed called jet streams, generally fastest at about 30,000 ft. Any one-jet stream does not extend all the way round the world so that the air can both enter and leave it.

When the air enters a jet stream is has to speed up a lot and for a time is going too slowly for the forces involved. By a nifty piece of physics it can be shown that this makes the air turn towards the left (in the Northern Hemisphere). So the air piles up, as it were, near the left-hand entrance to a jet stream and raises the pressure at all levels below this. On the right-hand side of the jet-entrance air has been removed and this, naturally, causes low pressure. At the exit of a jet stream the conditions are exactly the opposite, the air now moving too fast and turning to the right so that High and Low formation are reversed. The vital thing about these pressure changes is that in a High the "piled-up" air is slowly descending (it has nowhere else to go) whereas in a Low the air is ascending (the debit in the upper atmosphere has to be filled from somewhere). Now we can explain the characteristic weather of Highs and Lows. The descending air in a High is warmed by compression, and this warming lowers its relative humidity. Normally the descending air does not reach the surface but with warm cloud free air above us a hot day is on the cards, except in winter when the sun is too weak to heat things up much.

But then there will be night frost under the clear skies. In a Low things are just the opposite with the air rising, cooling by decompression and condensing out its water vapour. Even more importantly, most Lows are associated with warm and cold fronts. These boundaries between warm and cold air are the surface manifestation of the sharp

OF WEATHER

By Tudor Hughes

Low pressure brought heavy rain and frequent flooding during the autumn of 2000 as in this picture taken on the 22nd October at Ware, Hertfordshire, by Michael Skinner.

temperature differences that cause the jet streams. At a warm front the lighter warm air rides up over the cold air and cools as it rises, condensing out its water vapour into clouds and rain. At a cold front the cold air "noses in" under the warm air, again causing it to rise, cool and produce cloud and rain. Of course, in a High, the generally descending air suppresses any activity from fronts and they tend to die out.

Lows don't live very long. They give the atmosphere a good stir-up which tends to even out temperature differences so that the jet stream is temporarily no longer active and the mechanism of formation and maintenance ceases to work - until the next one, which may be only 36 hrs away in an unsettled spell. Highs, on the other hand, are more placid, have less effect on the general flow, move more slowly and are harder to shift. But they, too, move on or collapse eventually, taking with them their fine dry weather.

A roadside thermometer showing 56°C in Seville, Southern Spain August 2003.
Actually the air temperature was more like 46°C [115F], still oven like. Picture sent by Peter Rogers of Sevenoaks, Kent.

THE COLDEST PLACE IN EUROPE?

This picture : The floor of the ' kältepol'or Grünloch on the 20th August 2003. Only grasses normally growing in the tundra of Siberia can survive its severe winter cold.

Weather eye magazine has highlighted three outstanding frosty locations.
In issue 6 we looked at the editor's weather station in the Chipstead Valley, Surrey and compared it to Hertfordshire's Rickmansworth. In issue 13 we featured a place that is often mentioned on TV and Radio forecasts, Redhill in Surrey.
These are not the only examples and many more are known such as Houghall in county Durham, Newport in Shropshire, St. Harmon in Powys, Carnworth in Strathclyde and the grandfather of all cold spots Braemar in Highland. In these chilly places temperatures below minus 20C can occur, Newport recording minus 26.1C on the 10th January 1982, England's lowest. Whilst the all-time minimum of minus 27.2C goes to Braemar in February 1895 and January 1982 and equalled at Altnaharra [Highland] in December 1995.
But there is a place where the above values would be a fairly mild absolute yearly minimum and I do not mean somewhere north of the Arctic Circle. Weather eye paid a visit to a remarkable place known locally as 'The Kältepol' or Grünloch where the temperature regularly sinks below minus 50C. It is situated some 65 miles south west of the Austrian capital, Vienna.
The `Kältepol' is a doline, a saucer shaped basin in karst or limestone scenery. Its floor is about 250 metres across and lies 1280 metres above sea level, the rim being just over a kilometre wide and 150 metres higher. There is no outlet. Beyond the `Kältepol' the peaks rise to 1650 metres [around 5400 feet].

The route down from the Grünloch via the Lechnergraben looking towards the valley of the river Ybbs.

It is a fairly strenuous $2\frac{1}{2}$ hour climb from the Ybbs Valley near Lunz am See via the Lechnergraben to the rim of the doline. Our party of three reached the crest around 19.00hrs on the 20th August 2003 although it was after we had deliberately overshot the doline and paid a visit to the Ybbstaler Hut to the south for some welcome refreshment and a marvellous view. Back at the 'Kältepol' the floor was now in shadow, and the sky clear, a good time to test whether the 'Kältepol' or Grünloch was aptly named. On the rim the temperature measured 18C but it fell steadily as we entered the doline. On reaching the bottom there was a distinct chill, a mist was forming and it

The editor taking temperature readings on the floor of the doline.

Mist shrouds the frozen floor of the Grünloch in April 2002

BY IAN CURRIE

was only 9C and dropping. It fell a further degree over the 10-15 minutes exploring the floor but then we had to leave as already it meant a descent of the Lechnergraben in the gathering twilight.

This doline has been recognised for some time as being a truly remarkable place. The director of the Central Meteorological Institute of Vienna, Dr Schmidt, had established a meteorological station here during the 1930s and soon measured some quite outstanding readings.

For instance an absolute minimum of minus 52.7C [around minus 60F] was registered. On another occasion during a week in January 1930 a thermometer placed in Grünloch gave an absolute minimum of minus 26C yet on the ridge above the valley it did not fall below minus1C.

One morning in late March 1931 an incredible minus 45C was measured but a relatively mild minus 19C was recorded on the ridge.

During the Second World War the Grünloch was the scene of experimentation by German scientists on how fuels can be made to withstand low temperatures. In particular tank fuels for the Russian campaign.

The effect of such low temperatures on the vegetation can be seen in the photograph. Dense pine forests adorn the doline's sides but they become progressively thinner and more stunted towards the bottom of the basin and on the floor only grasses of the sort more commonly seen in the Siberian tundra flourish. Dr Schmidt was of the opinion that this locality could indeed experience the lowest temperatures in western and central Europe outside of northern Scandinavia.

Looking down on the Grünloch situated in the centre ground where the trees are absent. To the left is the approach via the Lechnergraben.

Picture by Bernard Pospichel. An excellent web site for detail on this remarkable place is www.lunz.at.tt

5

BUS OPERATION IN ALL WEATHERS

By Malcolm E Papes

Mv hobby over the years has been photographing and collecting old postcards of buses-or more specifically, as I am a geographer by training , of bus routes. I spent my first 18 years living near Pulborough in Sussex, and for much of that time went to school in Horsham which involved a long ride on Southdown Motor Services Ltd's route 69 twice a day. The company founded in 1915 is sadly no longer with us-first becoming part of the National Bus Company, and then, after a short reincarnation, being submerged as a subsidiary of Stagecoach Holdings.

Whilst conventionally photography of buses is best carried out in bright sunny weather, some pictures have been recorded in far from clement conditions. It might be added that in the earlier days, slow film speeds made it very difficult to capture a moving bus in less than brilliant sunshine, whilst snow on the ground would result in the camera overcompensating, and the bus turning out as underexposed. Nevertheless even in the earliest days pioneer photographers did go out in all weathers. The following black and white shots give us some idea of bus operation in less kindly conditions in Sussex.

1. Southdown Motor Services Ltd was formed on 1st April 1915 with vehicles from three concerns: Worthing Motor Services, London & South Coast Haulage Co, and Brigton,Hove and Preston United Omnibus Co.CD 1441 was a Straker-Squire chain driven U-type purchased by the latter company in 1911 It is seen here working for that company soon after delivery ploughing through floods at Shoreham on 6th November 1911 .The Brighton, Shoreham, Worthing route along the coast was one of the earliest. The poor surface of the roads even in the built-up areas and bad drainage made conditions like this common for these solid-tyred vehicles although the height of the body meant that they could get through quite deep flash flooding.

2.There was always something quaint about the radiator and body of these 32 seat singledeck Tilling Stevens buses which formed the rump of the saloon fleet in the late Twenties and Thirties. Some time in the Thirties, UF 6807,new in 1930,splashes across the flooded A29 just south of Pulborough at the widest section of the River Arun's floodplain. At this point it is called The Brooks, and the road,The Causeway. Route 69 linked Littlehampton with Horsham and it could expect to encounter conditions like this several times most winters. Indeed despite numerous drainage schemes, The Brooks still flood regularly although it takes rainfall such as that in the autumn of 2000 to cover the road itself. See issue 7.

3.This Southdown Leyland Titan TD5 with its body built to go under low bridges looks vulnerable to the huge waves which were battering the Promenade just to the west of Bognor Pier. Normally Southdown buses carried an attractive livery of apple green and cream, the entire roof and upper deck being in the latter. However, to make these buses less visible to the Luftwaffe, the light colours were replaced by grey and/or dark green for the duration of the War. This photograph of EUF 156 is likely to have been taken one stormy day very shortly after the War when access to the shore was derestricted, and the buses quickly regained their

4

peacetime livery.

4. Southdown doubledeckers were always vulnerable to gales from off the Channel. Perhaps the route at greatest risk was the busy 12 which operated along the coast road between Brighton and Easthourne over the exposed chalklands included the famous Seven Sisters. At times the service was diverted inland or suspended but squalls often blew up so quickly that such action was not anticipated. Leyland JCD 70 has come to grief one windy day in the early Fifties passengers having to escape by the rear upper deck emergency exit. The most spectacular incident of this kind occurred on the last day of 1948 when doubledecker 205 on route 10 was blown into the River Adur whilst crossing Old Shoreharn Toll Bridge. Amazingly there were no serious injuries as the tide was out and the bus fell onto the soft mud. A picture of this appears on page 79 of the Sussex Weather Book although unfortunately the date is wrong.

5. Until quite recently, Pool Valley in Brighton was the busiest of all Southdown bus stations with buses leaving the stands in the background for the town and all parts of Sussex and as far away as Portsmouth,Gravesend and Kent every minute or two. Originally Pool Valley had been a shallow inlet which had been drained before motor buses were invented. In the severe winter of 1962/63, a solitary Leyland on a local service is all that appears to be operating. A lone official is digging out the compacted snow at the narrow entrance. Icy roads and deep drifts virtually brought bus operations to a halt at the end of December and the first half of January in particular during this epic winter. Although located on the sunny South Coast, the downland to the east of Brighton made the town vulnerable to heavy snowfall.

2

1

3

Expressman Sutton Arrested as War Spy

"A Dover Express journalist probably got more front-page stories in national newspapers during the Second World War than anyone else in Britain. And all because of the weather!

When the war broke out, the government halted all up- to- date Weather news in British Newspapers in case they helped the enemy decide when to make an air raid or the best time to invade. All the newspapers accepted the rule, but in late 1940, after the fall of France, and with German troops only 21 miles away at Calais, an MP saw the stupidity of the Weather censorship rule. He pointed out that German observers on the cliffs at Calais could look across the water and know exactly what the weather was like in the Channel. The Government saw sense and gave permission for newspapers to report what the weather was like in the Dover Strait.

The task of reporting the weather to the national papers fell to reporter Norman Sutton who had a telephone installed at his Stanhope Road home especially for the job. The result as can be seen today in many yellowing wartime national newspapers, is Norman Sutton's daily front page weather report such as:" Overcast, sea choppy, foggy at night".

On one occasion Norman was "arrested" at gun-point whilst phoning his report from a phone kiosk. An over-zealous Army officer standing by the kiosk, heard the information being relayed, thought the man on the phone was a spy and pulled out his revolver to challenge Mr Sutton. The officer would not accept the explanation so Mr Sutton suggested they should go to the police station.

When they arrived the duty officers welcomed Norman whom they knew from his daily visits. They were highly amused at the arrest of the "spy"-and the embarrassed officer slunk away."

This news paper cutting from the Dover Express was kindly sent in by meteorologist Norman Brooks.

A Wartime advertisement. provided by Norman Brooks.

The glorious autumn of 2003. The sunny and dry conditions during the late summer and first half of the autumn enhanced the colours. Picture taken at The Nower near Headley, Surrey, 7th November by Ian Currie.

MEMORIES FROM A WEATHER ENTHUSIAST- PART 1: THE 1940s

BY PETER CLARKE

A mountainous snowdrift at Beaufort in Gwent, March 8th 1947.

With the approach of my 70th Birthday soon after Christmas the temptation to reminisce about one's early life is proving irresistible. So let me say straightaway that I have been an enthusiastic weather watcher for as long as I can remember!

For most of the first 20 years of my life I lived in Kingston, Surrey, or nearby in Teddington, Middlesex. Unfortunately I have no memory of the snowy Christmas of 1938 when I was a 4 year old but I certainly remember the cold January of 1940. My earliest recollection is of being taken by my mother to Kingston market to queue for eggs. A bitter east wind was blowing , the sun kept peeping out between fast moving clouds, and snow flakes fluttered down whisking about on the pavement. Many years later I visited the Met.Office Library at its HQ- then at Dunstable-and located the date as 10th January from its Daily Weather Reports for that month.

Both 1941 and 1942 produced cold snowy weather around the 10th January so, in 1943 (aged 9) I kept a daily weather diary from 1st January in the hope of being able to recognise the approaching cold weather. Unfortunately, this turned out to be a very mild winter and there was no January cold spell-and came as a surprise and a disappointment.

During World War 2 there were no broadcast weather forecasts (I was not even aware that forecasts were made) and no reports in the press or on the wireless of unusual weather events. This was because weather information might prove useful to the enemy. I came across books from the local library which contained some weather information and I gradually learned about cloud types and how thickening high cloud often preceded rain. This was my first forecasting clue and I soon picked up another one on my own: if north winds in winter bring clearing skies and night frosts, mild weather and rain will return within a couple of days.

February 1942 was a very cold month and I remember school milk being delivered to the classrooms and finding the contents of the bottles frozen. During a snowy day at about the same time, I was in a class room with high windows so it was difficult to see what was going on. I had already used up the excuse to visit the toilets so I had deliberately committed a minor misdemeanour (talking in class) which meant that culprits had to stand on the chair by their desk (I could then see out of the window). You had to be careful not to overdo the misconduct or you could find yourself sent to the Headmaster's study for further punishment.

May 8th, 1945(VE Day) was a date to relish. Not only did the war in Europe end, but listening to the morning news on the wireless the announcer said " Here, for the first time since 1939, is the Weather forecast". I was incredulous! The weather could be predicted! I still remember the forecast " It will be a warm day with thundery showers". It was correct and I remember naively thinking that all forecasts would be as good.

During my school days I found the autumns especially interesting- the dates of the first fogs and then the first frosts of the season were always keenly awaited. I carefully watched to see what time the morning fog cleared and, as the season advanced, the fogs lingered for longer.

The earliest date I remember a fog lasting all day was 30th October 1949 but usually it was mid November before they failed to clear. I used to think that if the fog persisted through the school "dinner hour" then it would last all day, provided the wind did not pick up or the sky clouded over. It was quite common for the persistent fogs to become much worse during the evenings.

Sometimes, visibility would be reduced to barely a few yards. Street lighting was not as efficient as today and on several occasions I remember walking along the pavement in the road where I lived and it was very difficult to find your own home. I used to stand by the fence or hedge at the front of the buildings and sometimes walk up to the front door to check on the house number. When you eventually located your home on entering the hall way it looked misty and the home smelt of fog.

The reason for these dense fogs was, of course, the smoke in the atmosphere. Almost every house was heated by a coal fire and it was not until after the Great Smog of December 1952 and the growth of both smokeless fuel and central heating that conditions began to improve.

Nowadays, radiation fogs are much less common and never as thick as those in the 1940s when, in the autumn, a spell of sunny weather with the wind falling light was invariably followed by a serious fog.

The highlight of my school days was the winter of 1946/47. After a pre-Christmas spell of cold east winds during the third week of December the weather became milder. There was another brief east wind spell from the 4th to the 7th of January but the wintry weather began in earnest on the 21st January. I remember cycling home from school and pedalling against a north east breeze, hoping that a new cold spell was starting! My chief memories of that winter were the frequent snowfalls, the lack of sunshine and the short-lived partial thaws. Sometimes, quite a lot of the snow melted but then the frost would return, the snow on the pavements and roads became icy (a hazard for cyclists!) and fresh snow soon covered everything again. The weather forecasts on the wireless were read by a studio newsreader and during this long cold spell usually ended with the words `Further outlook-wintry weather continuing'. The ground was at least partially snow covered from the 25th January to 8th March.

The summer of 1947 was memorable for its hot weather. August was almost rainless and very sunny but my main memory is going to Lord's cricket ground and seeing Denis Compton score several hundreds in an effortless and enthralling way. The summer weather continued through September and into October that year.

By this time I had a thermometer hanging on a shed in the garden and had received a barometer for my 12th birthday.

A snowy day at Malvern, Hereford and Worcester in February 1940 sent to us from Mr G. Johnson.

Postcard from the editor's collection- Crownest Park, Dewsbury, West Yorkshire, February 1940.

A Review of the

The first part of this article can be found in issue 12.

The 1990's warming was strongest in March, +1.7,and weakest in May, October and November at +0.1C. For 7 out of the 12 months the 90's was the warmest decade. The 40's, 50, and 60's produced the coldest decadal winter months. The coolest spring, summer and autumn months, were in the early decades of the century.

The notorious 60's did not just produce the great winter of 62/63,but the coldest decade for the months of March, July and December, although paradoxically the warmest Octobers.

Coldest Winters and Hottest Summers.

This table 5 shows the 5 coldest winters, taking the conventional Dec-Feb definition, but also looking at Jan/Feb and Jan/ March

	Dec-Feb	Jan-Feb	Jan March
1963	-0.33C	-1.47	1.07C
1947	1.13C	0.15C	1.30C
1917	1.47C	1.25C	1.90C
1940	1.47C	0.60C	2.40C
1979	1.57C	0.40C	1.83C

On all three criteria 1962/63 wins hands down. The persistence of cold in 1916/17 is apparent even if its Jan/Feb average is higher than the three winters of 1942 (0.5),1929 (0.8) and 1986 (1.2). In looking at summer the conventional June-August is taken, but in addition the average of the two hottest months July and August.

	June-Aug	July/Aug
1976	17.6	18.2
1995	16.6	18.9
1947	16.6	17.8
1933	16.6	17.7
1911	16.4	18.2

1976 produces the hottest 3 month period, but 1995 wins on the two months of high summer with 18.9°C.Two other summers produced Jul/Aug figures the same or above those in the top five,1955 with 17.9°C, and 1997 with 17.8°C.

Explanations for 20th Century Warming.

It is clear that although, not surprisingly , there is variation from decade to decade ,year to year and month to month, the key trend of the 20th century is one of warming. So is this normal cyclical variation or is there an underlining cause?

The conventional explanation is that this warming results from increased CO_2 emissions leading to a "greenhouse" effect, and evidence points increasingly to this being the major factor.

But what about other factors? In the 17th century sunspot activity was very low and this coincided with "a little ice age" in UK temperatures. So what has happened to sunspot activity in the 20th century?

The chart below shows the annual number of sunspots as a 12 year running mean to smooth out the effect of the 11 year sunspot cycles.

The graph shows the level rising dramatically in the 2nd

20th Century part 2:

By Roger Heape

half of the century compared to the early part. Annual average levels were only between 30 and 40 for the first 30 years. At the peak in the late 50's the values reached nearly 90 and climbed back again to these levels in the 90's.

Broadly the pattern for the century is low levels for the first 30 years, 30 years of increase from 1930-1960, a sharp drop in the 60's and early 70's and then a strong increase for the next 25 years.

It is difficult to correlate the absolute levels exactly with the decadal shifts in temperature, although the sharp fall of the 60's coincides roughly with the cooling pattern of CET, and the overall increase in activity mirrors the warming trend of the 20 th century.

Assuming that increase sunspot activity means extra energy received by the earth, it is likely to be reflected by sea temperature changes, which then feed through to atmospheric circulation.

The North Atlantic Oscillation.

This is an index which measures the variation from the average of sea surface pressure between the Azores and Reykjavik, Iceland. In broad terms big pressure differences and therefore positive anomalies suggest stronger west to east flow and stormier weather.

Low figures mean a slacker gradient and drier weather. There is a correlation between winter NAO values and temperatures although the link is less pronounced in summer.

Chart to show NAO annual indices for the 20th century expressed as 10 year running mean.

The overall picture shows positive values for most of the 20th century, with the exception of the 30 year period from the mid 50's to mid 80's. The pattern shows a low start, climbing strongly, and then a downward trend from around 1915 to a low in the late 60s, followed by a strong increase to the end of the century.

The pattern does not coincide with detailed temperature trends, but it does track the mid century cooling and subsequent warming.

Research suggests that in general there is some link between the NAO and sea surface temperature in the Atlantic but the exact links are not yet established However there is increasing confidence on the winter correlation so who knows in a few years time we may have advance warning of a big freeze like 62/63-that's if global warming doesn't rule them out altogether!

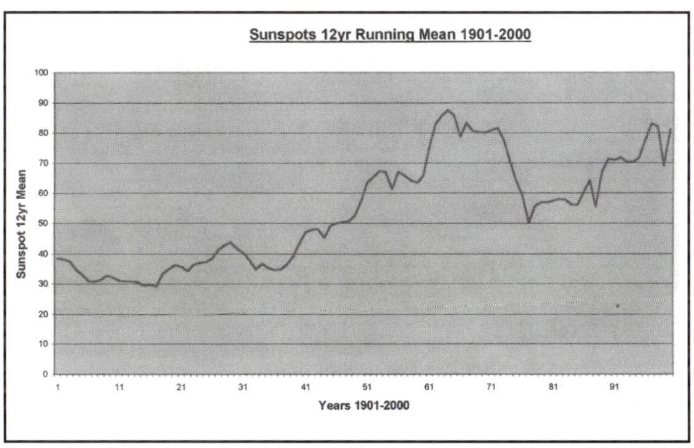

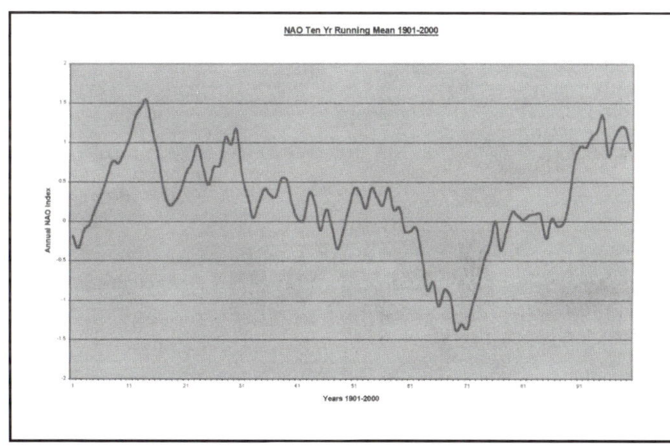

A decaying cumulonimbus cloud with virga trails beneath at sunset, Miami Beach, Christchurch, Barbados, October 2003. Picture by Selina Gilbert

HURRICANE FABIAN

GREETS NEW BERMUDA RESIDENTS

Before and After pictures courtesy of Fiona Lewis.

Fabian was the most powerful storm to hit Bermuda since Hurricane Edna in September 1953. It swept over the Atlantic island on Friday Sept 5th 2003 unleashing winds of 120 mph, felling trees and power lines and causing flooding in some areas.

Fabian hit Bermuda, which lies about 560 miles (900 km) east of South Carolina, as a Category 3 storm on the five-point Saffir-Simpson scale of hurricane intensity.

Weather eye received (from a subscriber Mrs Redshaw) an `on the spot' account of a close encounter with Fabian. It was sent to her from a friend who had very recently moved from England to Bermuda and described herself as a `hurricane virgin'. Just before the storm was expected to hit the island Mrs Redshaw received this email.

"We are all busy making preparations and have bought torches, candles, tape for the windows and we are stocked up on tins. Then it's a glance at the phone directory where there is a Bermudan guide to hurricane survival to make sure that all our preparations are complete and then start filling buckets of water before the power goes down. Up to now things have been very enjoyable with nice weather, lovely views, our house has even a private dock and beach".

After the storm struck Mrs Redshaw received another email and things were very different. Her friend wrote in breathless fashion, *"Ooh dear. Very windy, trees vanish, boats sink, roads buckle and roofs fly away. Four days after the storm husband still off work as building is smashed. Still no power; no cooker, fridge, water, lights and invaded by ants. No buses running and no car but we all survived and we love the place. It beats the M25."*

Attached to the email were two pictures showing how the peaceful view from her Bermudan garden had been changed.

RACING FEELING THE DROUGHT 2003

By A Vasquez

Left insert showing the almost empty reservoir at Wincanton in the spring of 2003 and main picture Wincanton Race course. Pictures courtesy of Wincanton race course.

The drought which affected much of England for several months caused more than its fair share of problems for Horse Racing, its racecourses and the horses themselves.

One racecourse, Wincanton in Somerset was even forced to abandon its first jumping fixture of the season because the ground was too firm and its reservoir bone dry. Back to Wincanton later.

It is important to appreciate that the underfoot conditions or 'going' as it is known in racing parlance, is the single most important deciding factor affecting how a racehorse will perform in his race, as well as being crucial to the horses' safety and long term welfare.

Individual racehorses inherit likes and dislikes regarding 'going' in the same way as human beings' traits are handed down from their parents. Some horses will prefer racing on soft or heavy ground whereas others will like a firmer surface. Underfoot conditions de-scribed as 'good' are generally accepted as the perfect 'happy medium'.

Unfortunately, racehorses' physique is not conducive to racing on really firm ground whatever their likes or dislikes. The average weight of a racehorse is half a ton, and that sort of weight coming down on fragile forelegs can cause soreness, or worse still can cause a horse to 'break down' or go lame. During this very hot and dry Summer, racecourses have been relentlessly watering their courses from their own bore holes and reservoirs to provide safe racing conditions; after all, half a ton of racehorse travelling at 40 mph can make a considerable impact on the turf.

However, it is during the National Hunt or Jumping season where the weather can really cause problems as the most competitive and best jumpers race during the winter months when problems are normally caused by frost and water logging and not drought. Jumping stiff fences and hurdles at average speeds of around 30 mph can put its own special demands on horses' legs, so underfoot conditions with plenty of ease in them are absolutely essential.

Back to Wincanton then. Their first fixture of the current season on October 9th was reluctantly abandoned. The Course's reservoir was empty, and the racecourse Executive dis-covered it would cost them £12,500 to purchase a quantity equivalent to an inch or 25mm of rain on the course. It seems that 2 inches would have been required to provide suitably safe racing conditions. The outlay of £25,000 in order to put on a one-day meeting was not financially viable, so unfortunately the meeting had to fall by the wayside.

In a very similar situation, Cheltenham Racecourse, the Mecca of steeple chasing, decided to purchase 5 million gallons of water from the Severn Trent Water Authority in order to water their ground so that the 28th/29th October Meeting went ahead. Their reservoir iswas extremely low and persistent watering failed to move the 'going" from hard to firm. The dry weather caused problems for two other high profile racecourses. The 2 day Flat Race Meeting at Ascot on 26 and 27 September worth hundreds of thousands of pounds in prize money went ahead all right but was hit by many trainers withdrawing their horses because of the firm ground. The Racecourse had plenty of water to put on the track and with the meeting due to commence on the Friday, they started to water on the Monday prior to racing. However, the Met. Office forecast significant rain for the area on Friday so Ascot stopped watering for fear of creating bog like conditions.

The rain failed to materialize by which time it was too late to recommence watering, hence the mass withdrawal of runners. An identical situation arose a week later at New-market. This course retain John Ketley as a weather adviser. Mr. Ketley forecasted significant rain for the Newmarket area; so the course ceased watering. However the rain failed to arrive so racing took place on firmer conditions than des-irable. Whether Mr. Ketley is still retained by Newmarket as their weather advisor is not known!

So with the jumping season just beginning to get com-petitive with its climax next March at the Cheltenham Festival followed by the Grand National Meeting at Aintree in early April it is to be hoped that proper rain falls during the winter.* Racing is a multi-million pound industry and one of the largest employers in the country. It is used to the normal winter problems provided by freezing conditions and water logging, but not drought. Incidentally, Wincanton's meeting on October 26th went ahead thanks to the purchase of a considerable amount of water and racing also took place on November 8th. However on both occasions there were very few runners due to the firm ground. Taunton racecourse was even worse off. They cancelled both their 16th and 30th October meetings and November 13th was a non-starter as well.

Nobody could remember the ground so dry in mid autumn.

** It has for many in the south during 20th/23rd Nov when many places measured over 70mm of rain in 48 hrs. The Newton Abbot Racecourse, had it's meeting cancelled due to waterlogging.*

Competition winners issue 13

Congratulations to Caroline Foster of Southwater in West Sussex for winning the book 'The Greatest Storm' by Martin Brayne'. Mr Kevin Doxey of Renishaw received a runner up prize of ' The Weather of 90s ' by Peter Wright. Mr John Cunningham of Old Coulsdon received a copy of the 'Barometer Manual' by Robert Fitzroy.

The answer to the competition of who was on the throne at the time of the 1703 storm is Queen Anne.

WHY NOT TRY THE ISSUE 14 COMPETITION, THE PRIZE IS A COPY OF THE COLLINS GUIDE *HOW TO ID THE WEATHER* BY STORM DUNLOP. IT NORMALLY COSTS £12.99 TO BUY AND IS LAVISHLY ILLUSTRATED WITH OVER 180 COLOUR PICTURES.

SIMPLY SEND IN YOUR HUMOUROUS WEATHER PICTURE, like this one from Mrs Davison from Hook, Surrey capturing a novel use for a wind vane. Runner up prizes will also be given.

Pictured below:
A spectacular cold front clearance as it moves away eastwards from Shrewsbury, May 18th 2003.
Taken by Mr D Corbin.

HEATWAVE BRINGS THE CLAIMS

by Malcolm Johnson

In the last issue of Weather eye, mention was made of the thunderstorms that affected areas of the country on 20th June and the spell of hot weather that was beginning to generate excitement amongst meteorologists. Since then the United Kingdom temperature record has been broken, with 38.5C-(101 .3F) being reached at Brogdale, near Faversham, Kent and although temperatures subsequently dropped to a more tolerable level little rain fell until the end of October. As a result, insurance companies received a wide range of claims for damage caused by these extreme conditions.

The June thunderstorms damaged houses and their contents with personal computers being a frequent casualty. Modems seemed to be particularly vulnerable and one company in Gillingham, Dorset found itself having to deal with calls from most of its customers.

On 8th August 2003, I dealt with a claim at Brockenhurst, Hampshire caused by some fairly hefty branches of a Scots Pine tree falling and hitting fencing and a greenhouse. A couple of days later Ian Currie received reports of trees falling at Buckingham and Reigate. I am quite sure there have been other examples and it would seem that the high temperatures and lack of moisture proved catastrophic in such cases.

When the hot weather was at its peak, temperatures remained high in roof spaces and I dealt with a number of cases where pipes split apart at joints, or ballcocks failed resulting in water cascading through houses causing significant damage.

At the end of August I was called to look at a property in Ramsgate, Kent where an area of the lath and plaster ceiling at the top of the stairs had crumbled and fallen, but the policyholder was unable to work out the reason why it had occurred. She told me that she had discovered the damage upon returning from a two-week holiday and that the property had been shut up while she and her family had been away. My conclusion was that the high temperatures and lack of ventilation had dried the plaster to such a degree that there was no longer sufficient adhesion and down it had come.

Such claims though are but a very small fraction of those caused by the dry, hot weather. They pale into insignificance when compared to the volumes of subsidence claims received. As in previous dry summers, the peak time for problems to be reported is September and October when the shrinkage of the clay subsoil reaches its peak. Structural engineers and surveyors will be engaged either by policyholders or the insurance companies direct to inspect the damage and commence a long period of monitoring to determine whether, as winter rainfall increases the moisture content of the subsoil, the cracks close up again. If extraction of moisture from the subsoil by trees has had an effect it will be necessary to decide whether the tree should either be pruned or felled, which coupled with the winter rainfall should help the situation. If the cracks do close up, then insurance companies will simply pay for repairing the cracks and redecorating, but if the cracks do not close, or increase in size then it may be necessary to pay for the costly exercise of underpinning. Repairing subsidence damage is not to be rushed into and it is something for which insurers and surveyors wish that very accurate long- range weather forecasting was available!

The hot weather produced other difficulties too. For example roads built on clay subsoils cracked, railway tracks buckled (or at least threatened to, which is why blanket speed restrictions were imposed in August) and there was an increase in the death rate-2000 more than the average between 4 and 13 August.

Editor's note: The busy A3 road in Guildford, Surrey was badly affected by subsidence. Also my mother-in law living near Buckingham had to have a thirsty willow tree removed from her garden even though it was some way from the house. The roots had spread through the heavy clay soil and were partly responsible for cracks reappearing on the house walls after previous extensive work had been carried out after the very dry spell of 1995/96.

Just as the temperature reached its peak on the 10th August 2003 a large tree suddenly crashed down onto the busy A217 at Reigate, Surrey. This was one of a number of trees that toppled due to the record breaking heat.

Weather eYe

ISSUE 12

'GRIDLOCK THURSDAY' - 30th Jan 2003

'STORMY SUNDAY' - 27th Oct 2002

MARCH 'MANY WEATHERS'

Weather eye

"For everyone fascinated by the Weather."

From the Editor

A big thank you to all of you for providing such an array of Weather pictures and articles for issue 12. The Jekyll and Hyde month of January produced many weather events and has made Weather eye slightly delayed so we could do justice to all your material from floods to snowstorms. Please keep on sending in pictures and articles. They are the lifeblood of Weather eye. If there is an interesting Weather event, sky formation or meteorological conundrum near you why not write about it or capture it on film and we could feature it. Also thanks to those of you who sent in answers to issue 11's competition. The winners are on page 11 and there is a new challenge that I hope many of you will try. If you would like an attractive plastic wallet enabling you to store up to 10 of your issues we can provide them at a cost of 3 for £2.50 including postage. Send cheques to Frosted Earth or add it to the cost when you renew your subscription. There is a slight increase to the subscription price for 3 issues of 25p to cover increased costs such as postage so it is now £6.75. Renewal for 6 issues though is a special rate of just £12.50. May I wish everyone a cloud nine time for the rest of 2003.

On the 29th December 2002 part of the West Pier, Brighton, collapsed. It was partly due to the weather conditions as winds had reached 50 mph and heavy rain had fallen but a lot to do with the pier being derelict for many years. Editor Ian Currie was there late in the day. It was remarkably mild with the mercury at 13C and a similar dew point. Perhaps the most amazing aspect witnessed was seeing how foolhardy people can be. Darkness was descending rapidly and powerful waves armed with masses of shingle were crashing onto the foreshore yet people were running into the water to get pieces of wreckage for souvenirs. One person came away with a window frame, another with a complete door. Others had some floor boards. Anyone of them could have been swept out to sea. This stunning picture was taken on a quieter day some weeks later by Robert Vanko.

Published by: Frosted Earth, 77 Rickman Hill, Coulsdon, Surrey CR5 3DT. ***Printed by:*** Litho Techniques Ltd, 46-50 Godstone Road, Whyteleafe, Surrey CR3 0EA

STORMY SUNDAY - 27TH OCTOBER 2002.

A deepening depression moved from southern Ireland across England and into the North Sea. On its southern flank especially over the south Midlands and into East Anglia winds were particularly strong for inland sites. Heathrow recorded 74 mph with similar speeds at Luton. At the Needles on the Isle of Wight a gust of 102 mph was recorded and 96 mph was measured at Mumbles in South Wales. Eight people, among them three children, were killed. Airports and roads were closed, ferry services suspended and power supplies to more than 100,000 homes cut.

David Mutton a regular contributor to Weather eye takes up the story: "At my weather station in Cosby, Leicestershire, the top gust was 72mph at 10.45hrs. The wind flow chart illustrated shows the gusts throughout the 24 hours of the 27th. These storm- force winds caused widespread damage across Leicestershire with fallen trees across roads and power lines. Many villages were without power for up to five days. A number of buildings were damaged. It was the highest wind speed in Cosby since 78 mph on the 4th January 1998".

Much of the transport network was thrown into confusion. British Airways cancelled 39 flights from Heathrow and Gatwick, and another 30 flights due out of Stansted were abandoned. The Queen Elizabeth II Bridge over the Thames at Dartford was closed, as was the Severn Bridge carrying the M48. Railway services were cancelled as fallen trees and damaged power cables forced line closures with an unusually large leaf fall exacerbating the problem on some lines. This was to delay trains over the following days. The Port of Dover was closed and ferry services cancelled. In

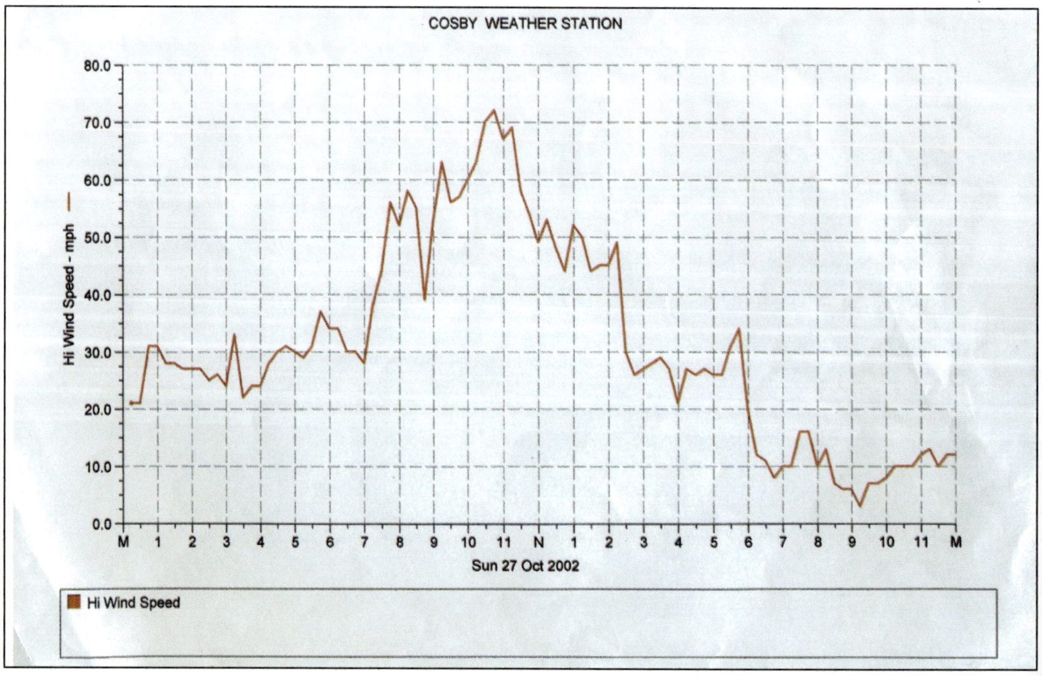

Left: A large horse chestnut branch being removed from a car in Warwick Avenue, Melton Mowbray, Leicestershire. Picture: Dave Mutton

This picture: The road into White Notley, Essex, blocked by fallen trees that brought down power lines as well. Picture by Philippe Hays.

Portsmouth the Navy's newest warship, the frigate St Albans, was seriously damaged when it was hit by a P & O ferry blown off course. A car ferry was unable to dock at Harwich and hundreds of passengers in the Admiral of Scandinavia had to endure a roller coaster day in the open water.

The storm brought controversy in its wake. Although it had been well forecast some power companies found it difficult to cope and even 5 days after the gale subsided 20,000 householders had still not been reconnected, 17,000 of them in East Anglia. Many people could not contact their suppliers for information as the call centres were overloaded. On a lighter note The Army appealed for help from the public after an inflatable tank was blown away shortly before an exercise was due to take place. It was one of six borrowed from the RAF and was attached to the ground with guy-lines that broke from their moorings at Trefil near Tredegar, Gwent.

"CHERTSEY'S NIGHTMARE LAUNCH INTO 2003."

Over a hundred and fifty homes evacuated

by Mark Davison

Paddocks Way,Chertsey underwater at the beginning of 2003. Picture courtesy of the Surrey Herald

THE floods to hit Southern England during an exceptionally wet period from November 2002 to January 2003 were the worst in living memory for some people living near the River Thames in Surrey. During the last 10 days of December places along the North Downs in Surrey measured over 120 - 130mm [5 inches] of rain and this made its way down river valleys such as the Wey towards the Thames. On the 30th alone up to 45mm [1.8 inches] of rain fell.

Chertsey, in the north west of the county, suffered damage estimated at more than £1million and dozens of householders had still not returned to their flooded homes in February. One hundred and fifty eight properties in and around the town were evacuated after the swollen rivers Bourne and Thames burst their banks. The nightmare for the residents started on New Year's Day when some 112 families were evacuated in Chertsey and another 46 from homes in nearby Egham.

Paddocks Way.
Picture courtesy of the Surrey Herald

Family in flood: Alison Greaney, Barbara Greaney and Laura Matthew in their flooded lounge at Chertsey. Courtesy of the Surrey Herald

Owners of riverside homes in Shepperton were advised to leave while others in Chertsey's Docket Eddy could only depart by boat.

Many people in unaffected properties tried to acquire sandbags from Runnymede Council but only emergency requests were granted. Some people blamed the catastrophe on clogged rivers and irresponsible building developments in the flood plain. Chertsey Cricket Club at one stage considered suing the Environment Agency for bad advice. Estate agents in the area were forecasting a drop in house prices. One agent told the Surrey Herald newspaper: "It is devastating for people whose homes have been flooded because insurance premiums will rocket. When a similar flood hit Byfleet two years ago, homes could not be sold for at least a year". But sales of wellington boots at a store in Addlestone were up tenfold.

The newspaper had predicted in 2001 that the Bourne was at risk from further flooding because of the amount of discarded junk such as supermarket trolleys, tyres, 'fridges' and mattresses in the water and on the banks. Paddocks Way in Chertsey took the brunt of the flooding. Fire-fighters used dinghies to rescue people. Mother-of-two Sarah Dillen, 35, said: "I spent Christmas in hospital and had been home for two days when my living room was turned into a huge indoor pool. It all happened so quickly. I couldn't believe it. The electricity went off and we were under water within a couple of hours. I just want to go to sleep and wake up and it's 2004." In Thames Ditton, the RNLI in two craft assisted with the evacuation of householders from Thames Ditton Island. The water level of the Thames near the Swan Public House was higher than at any time during the major autumn 2001 floods, but the water receded just before it reached the bars. Shopkeepers in Thames Ditton village, however, suffered badly. Floodwater entered several properties including a sports equipment shop and geysers of water sprung persistently from manhole covers along the High Street for several days.

Over 109mm of rain in the last week of December 2002 triggered several landslides in the deep railway cuttings on the Brighton railway line between Coulsdon and Merstham. Around midday on January 1st 2003 a train carrying over 100 passengers narrowly avoided disaster when it was derailed but managed to stay up right. It was travelling slowly due to speed restrictions imposed by previous rock falls. See issue 8 page 3. Picture Ian Currie

Storm Surge Jan/Feb 1953

by Ian Currie

As a whist drive was in progress at a Nissen Hut used fo a village hall at Sea Palling, Norfolk, the sea swept through the community. Seven people were drowned here during this night of terror. Picture from Norfolk and Suffolk Weather Book. 'Ogly, Davidson and Currie'

On the last day of January 1953 a deepening area of low pressure moved from the north west of Scotland towards Denmark and brought about one of Britain's worst weather disasters. It was in stark contrast to earlier in the winter when London and other urban areas were under the influence of high pressure and shrouded in a dense smog.

A depression deepened to 964 millibars in the North Sea just off the east coast of Scotland at 06.00hrs on the 31st. It had a very steep pressure gradient in its wake producing a potent and destructive gale.

For instance at 06.00 hrs on the 31st there was a 32mb gradient in surface pressure from the Outer Hebrides to Wick. An anemometer at Costa Hill, Orkney measured a wind gust of 126mph and a mean speed of 90 mph. At Lossiemouth 108 mph was recorded. It claimed the lives of 133 people sailing on the ferryboat Princess Victoria which foundered in tumultuous seas off Stranraer. On land many thousands of trees were toppled across Scotland and overall 5 per cent of the total standing coniferous timber in the UK was destroyed. The fierce wind with a long sea track forced some 420,000 million cubic metres of water from the Atlantic to the North Sea coinciding with a high spring tide. The sea surface also rose as a result of the drop in pressure and as night closed in the 31st a force of unimaginable power swept a wall of water southward into the bottleneck of the southern North Sea.

Mere facts such as King's Lynn recorded a high tide 2.5 metres greater than predicted or at Southend the sea was 2 metres above the expected height for 15 consecutive hours give very little idea of the horror suffered by tens of thousands of people during that fateful night. Between the Tees and Dover the boiling sea overtopped or breached a network of sea defences. The first thing many people knew of the danger was the smashing down of their front doors by a surging current of icy seawater. In a frenzy of splitting timber and splintering glass it tossed furniture aside and engulfed houses to the ceiling. In places such as Canvey Island many people drowned in their beds whilst others fought with superhuman effort against terrible currents in inky darkness to reach their rooftops. Over 300 square miles were totally engulfed by the sea and 307 people lost their lives.

Names such as Mablethorpe, King's Lynn, Hunstanton, Felixstowe, Jaywick, Canvey Island became synonymous with death, destruction yet sublime heroism. The desolate scenes were vividly described by a BBC correspondent who flew over Essex. In emotional voice his broadcast was relayed to a stunned nation,

"Canvey Island bits of furniture, belongings floating absolute desolation-And then we flew over Foulness-just the tops of farms, roofs of barns and a boat caught in a tree top, people struggling to get clear-a heap of caravans thrown together in Jaywick- a deserted village". One man told of reaching a tree and finding it full of screeching rats.

At Tilbury 2,500 of the town's 2,750 houses were flooded, some immersed in 2 metres of water. 10,000 people were forced to remain in upstairs rooms. No costs can be adequately placed on human life. But in insured losses to property, infrastructure, transport etc in today's value the 1953 Event would top £15,000 million pounds at least. It was said at the time that the sea's achievement in one night challenges comparison with that of the Luftwaffe in six years.

It was obvious that there were serious shortcomings to sea defences and to communications. Why was news of the frightening surge in Lincolnshire and Norfolk heading south not relayed to authorities in Essex? In the immediate aftermath some 30,000 people put to work to repel the sea but in the long term a Storm Tide Warning Service for the whole of the east coast in conjunction with the Admiralty's hydrographic department and the Met. Office was created. In 1984 the Thames Flood Barrier was completed drastically reducing the likelihood of the capital being flooded. The horrific events of that terrible night in 1953 were an awful reminder as to the immense power of Nature in malevolent mood.

The beacon lit over the Weekend at the beginning of February 2003 on the approach to Canvey- Essex as a remembrance to those who died on the island 50 years ago. The inset picture shows the permanent memorial plaque outside the library.

A bore or aegir rushing upstream at Gainsborough, Lincolnshire on the river Trent.

BORES AND AEGIRS

by Ian Currie

The Weather can play a part in creating one of the strangest spectacles seen on some our river systems. Aegirs or bores can make quite a splash. "Eagre" is the Old English word for a flood or full tide. They are well known on the rivers Severn, Wye, Humber, Trent and Ouse. The incoming tide is momentarily checked by the downstream river current and the water rears up and then heads up stream as one large wave of a series of smaller ones. It is when there is a very high tidal range that prominent bores can occur. The river Severn has the second highest tide in the world up to 15 metres has been recorded and it sweeps in across the exposed sands of the estuary at over 10-mph. The word "bore" is from the Old Scandinavian bora and it means a wave. It can be quite a dramatic sight and is best seen below Gloucester on the Severn. It is a fascinating occasion to see the river flow suddenly reverse. Most of the year's bores are unspectacular but each year some may reach 2 metres in height. There are a number of influences that can affect the size of the bore with the Weather playing its part. Firstly, the height and speed of the tide which is trying to enter the narrowing and shelving estuary varies through the lunar month. The highest tides follow a few days after new and full moons and the largest 50 bores of the year occur in the periods February to April and August to October, around the spring and autumn equinoxes. The record height is nearly 3 metres [9 feet]. Other influences are the amount of fresh water in the river, the atmospheric pressure and, finally, the direction of the wind. Strong winds from the west or south-west out in the Atlantic Approaches will increase the bore's height. The tide is the most important of these influences but while tides can be predicted with great accuracy, the result of the mix of all four factors cannot. The result is that you can easily check when a bore will occur but you cannot be sure how spectacular it will be. It can be quite a shock for the unwary mariner and boats that are not tied correctly can be torn from their moorings. Listen out for the shout " Tide Ho!" Friday April 18th could be a good day in 2003 to witness the Severn bore at Minsterworth around 09.56 hrs. but a couple of days before and after could be good viewing as well. On the Trent it is best seen at Littleborough in Nottingham. For places to see the bore on the Severn an excellent web site is **www.severnbore.ndirect.co.uk** by Chris Witts.

GRIDLOCK THURSDAY

Snowfalls of Thursday January 30th 2003

By Mark Davison

Evening Standard

LONDON, FRIDAY, 31 JANUARY 2003

NEWS EXTRA

40p

GRIDLOCK

WHO'S TO BLAME?

FULL DRAMATIC STORY ON PAGES 2, 3, 4 AND 5

IN HISTORICAL terms, the snow that swept Southeast England on Thursday January 30th 2003 was not exceptional. In places, it exceeded three inches [8cm] in depth and, unusually, was deeper in many parts of London and Middlesex than over the North Downs in Surrey and Kent. But it was the complete traffic dislocation that will make it a weather event to remember and came just 72 hours after the warmest ever January day in the South east with 17.4C measured at East Malling in Kent and 16C exceeded widely. Cars, lorries and buses were trapped in gridlock conditions on main roads across a wide area of North London, Essex, Cambridgeshire and Hertfordshire for up to 20 hours. A six-mile journey on the A10 from Cheshunt to Hertford took from 6pm until midnight. Those stuck included a group of partygoers who were heading for the Marriott Hotel in Hertford. They set off in a small convoy of cars soon after 5.30pm with the intention of raising a glass to a colleague's new job, but failed to reach the hotel until after midnight by which time the celebrations were over. They sat in their cars hardly moving and the snow was falling thickly until it eased off at about 10.30pm, only to resume in the early hours of the next day. The passengers kept their spirits up by sending text messages to their friends and speaking on their mobile phones. The M11 motorway through Cambridgeshire and Essex was jammed solid with stationary traffic all evening and night. Schoolchildren on one bus were trapped for 18 hours and local villagers arrived with food supplies. Elsewhere, one driver took a box of crisps along a queue, handing out packets. Another six-mile journey to Mill Hill, North London, took in excess of eight hours, as did a journey from Elstree to Hampstead. People all over the region said that the main problem was that concerning toilets. In North London, there were reports of road rage as frustrated drivers lost their tempers trying to find out in vain what was going on.

Throughout the night, local radio stations such as LBC tried to keep drivers informed of the situation and for many, this was the only way people could glean any information of how, if at all, they were likely to get home. There was a noticeable lack of announcements from any Home Counties' police force over the air.

Snow has been so limited in recent winters over many parts of the South it caught some people by surprise as in this East Grinstead garden on the 4th January 2003. Picture by Alan Cullen

Many London children had not experienced a significant fall of snow but a thick cover provided much enjoyment on the 8th January 2003. Here Jake Davison is enjoying a heavy fall at Addington Golf Course, Croydon. He was able to revel in another one on the 30th January 2003 when London's traffic became grid-locked. Picture Nigel Davison.

At 8am on Friday a stranded motorway driver told an incredulous LBC presenter: "I have been here since four o'clock this afternoon". One public house in Wembley welcomed in a large group of marooned drivers and offered them hot food. Another in the area cared for a party of schoolchildren who had been going nowhere in their mini-bus since 4pm. At 8.30am next morning, a woman who had been stuck on the M11 since 5pm the previous evening said she was "cold, scared, and almost out of fuel."

A woman who was six months' pregnant had to spend all night on the M11 in her car. Charlotte Lamont said it was "very difficult to get comfortable" and she feared

Metro Bus 404 on the 161 route battling through the snow at Chislehurst, Kent on the south-east edge of London on the 8th January 2003. Picture by John King.

what would have happened had she required an ambulance. She had to suffer the embarrassment of using the side of the road as a lavatory. A lorry driver took pity on all the hungry drivers around him. Alex Maclean, who was also trapped on the M11, spoke to his bosses at Hazelwood Sandwiches who approved his request to share out the cargo of snacks.

At Brent Cross, North London, 500 shoppers were stranded by the weather. Waitrose supplied food and drink while Boots gave out free nappies for six babies.

One unlucky traveller stuck in a taxi on the M11 was presented with a fare of £212. Near Newmarket, Suffolk, irate motorists on the A414 took out tools and, with difficulty, unbolted the central reservation so they could escape in their vehicles down the opposite carriageway. A witness said: "It was like a dam had burst. Everyone started using the hole."

The main television news was not about the Iraq crisis, but concerned the traffic chaos - the worst ever known in the Southeast. Why were the roads not gritted? Were councils trying to save money? Who was to blame? The snow had been predicted as early as Sunday and ample warnings had been given. Many local authorities and the Highways Agency, which is responsible for gritting arterial routes and motorways, gave a variety of reasons. They included the wrong timing of the snow; traffic congestion preventing gritting lorries from doing the job; and a multitude of accidents blocking roads. Some boroughs, including Southwark, had been gritting roads constantly since the day before the Thursday snows, while in Ealing, West London, lorries were not out until 4pm on Thursday. Questions were asked at Westminster and inquiries were promised. Transport Secretary Alistair Darling said he had demanded answers from the road, rail and local authorities. "Snowfall in January is hardly unexpected," he told reporters. There was further widespread disruption on the railways. At West Hampstead, North London, passengers were asked to leave a train and walk along the snow-covered tracks to safety. However, hundreds of railway staff had worked through the night to try and keep the trains running and help customers get home. London Underground said de-icing fluid sprayed onto rails was washed off by melting snow. It was estimated that the turmoil could have cost business at least £150million as thousands could not get to work and supplies failed to get through. Thousands of homes in Eastern England were without power for up to 24 hours. Most of the chaos was in the evening when blizzard-like snow showers moved in from the North Sea, particularly affecting the east of the region and the counties to the north and north west of London. However, the day had dawned with a separate band of snow moving in from the west which hit the western parts of Surrey and northeast Hampshire just in time for the morning rush hour. Schools in Farnborough, Camberley and Farnham closed after staff and pupils were unable to get in. Roads in Farnborough were particularly affected and the Hogs Back route was closed near the Blackwater Valley. Yet in the east of the county, around Reigate and Dorking, only the lightest dusting was reported until later in the day when the snow arrived on high winds from the north east. As the gusts increased in strength, a tragedy occurred at Ashtead, near Leatherhead, Surrey, when a tree came crashing down on a school playground at West Ashtead Primary School, killing an eight-year-old girl, Rianna Davenport, and injuring two other pupils. Rescue workers toiled away in falling snow to release the trapped pupils.

KENT SNOW LAMENT

By Stephen Wintle of Ashford, Kent.

The north wind did blow
But it still did not snow;
Then veered to the east
But we only got sleet.

While Kent could not muster a smidgen of snow,
The rest of The Kingdom had plenty to show.
The Northeast of England had thirty feet drifts;
[The snow-loving Geordies o'erjoyed with these gifts]
While Scotland saw blizzards that were so severe,
They might not be repeated for hundreds of years.

Snowdonia proudly lived up to its name,
And the Isle of Wight had a similar refrain;
While even on Scilly they'd enough for a sledge.
Much more of this and I'll be over the edge!

The Garden of England stayed stubbornly green,
But the mainland of Europe wore a silvery sheen;
All sparkly and glistening, resplendent in ice,
A winter sensation, a white paradise.

It snowed in the East, it snowed in the West,
From St. Petersburg down to Bordeaux and Trieste;
The Rhine and the Rhône became stagnant and froze
As the temperature dropped to near forty below;
And the Baltic iced up to unparalleled depths,
So nothing at all for the fishermen's nets.

It fell in the Costas where gold turned to white,
In Athens and Tunis, [a very rare sight];
Majorca and Rome saw significant falls,
While snow could be glimpsed from Jerusalem's walls;
There were even reports of a dusting in Crete,
But in Kent only mud would get under our feet

Oh merciful spirits, please send me some snow
If I don't get some soon I'll be ten feet below!

Editor's Note:
In spite of some significant falls in north Kent during January, Ashford still managed nothing more than a thin veneer.

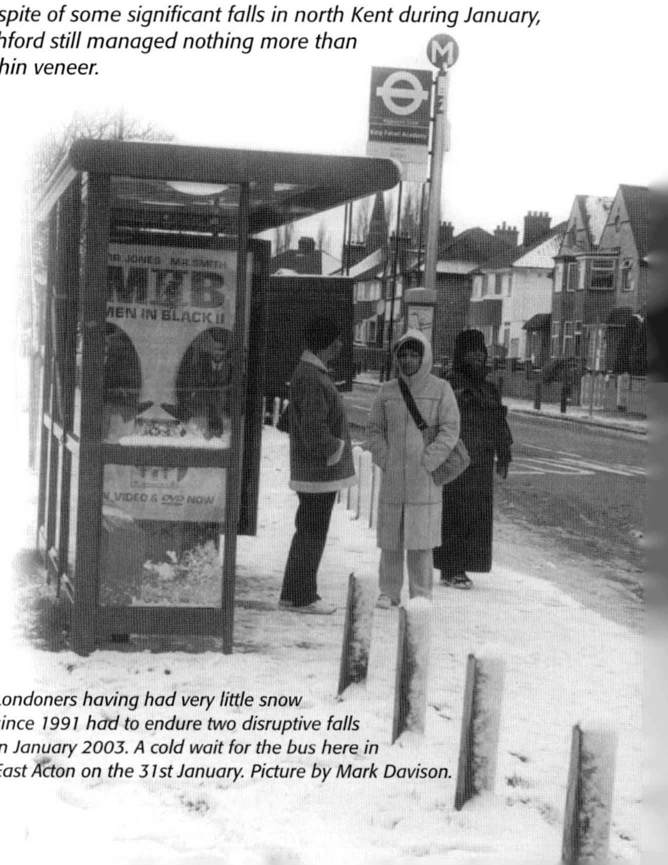

Londoners having had very little snow since 1991 had to endure two disruptive falls in January 2003. A cold wait for the bus here in East Acton on the 31st January. Picture by Mark Davison.

A REVIEW OF 20th CENTURY CENTRAL ENGLAND TEMPERATURE TRENDS.

Part 1 By Roger Heape (BA Geography. Cantab 1967)

The 20th Century saw an increase of 1°C in CET* temperature. But what does this hide? Did winter warm up faster than summer? Which month warmed most and which least? Which decades and years were the hottest and coldest? Global warming resulting from increased Co2 emissions is given as the main explanation for the 20th century temperature rise , but has increased sunspot activity contributed and what about the vagaries of the North Atlantic Oscillation[NAO]?

Trends in Annual Average

There was an increase of 1°c between the coldest and warmest decades of the century. Coincidentally these were the first and last decades. The smoothed ten year running means (Fig .1) show that this increase was not uniform. The pattern shows the well documented warming to the end of the 40's followed by cooling during the 20years 1950-1970,and then warming for the last 30 years ,particularly pronounced in the1990's.

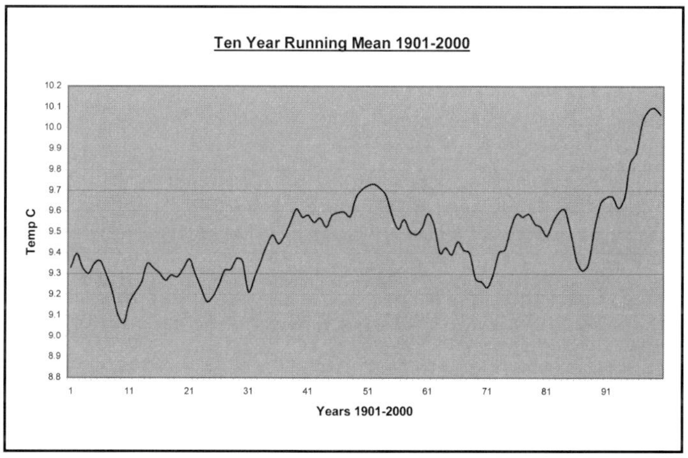

*Central England Temperature Series See Issue 5 page 3

Decadal Patterns in Annual Average.

The coldest decade was the first of the century, perhaps surprising as it contains no severe winters. It did however have cool springs and summers. Its annual average of 9.07°c, compares to the 10.06°c of the 90's. Average Variation from average

	Average °c	Variation from average
1901-1910	9.07	-0.44
1911-1920	9.33	-0.17
1921-1930	9.33	-0.14
1931-1940	9.57	0.07
1941-1950	9.71	0.21
1951-1960	9.52	0.02
1961-1970	9.26	-0.24
1971-1980	9.53	0.03
1981-1990	9.64	0.14
1991-2000	10.06	0.56

Comparing decades to the century average, aside from the 90's, the 1940's represented the warmest decade being 0.2°c above average. The coldest decade , outside the first was the 60's,-0.24°c below average.

Seasonal Changes.

Has the warming been uniform across the seasons? Table 2 shows the 90's temperature versus the average, and versus the coldest and warmest decades for each season.

	WINTER		SPRING		SUMMER		AUTUMN	
	Decade	Temp	Decade	Temp	Decade	Temp	Decade	Temp
Coldest Decade	60's	3.5	00's	8.0	00's	14.8	10's	9.5
Warmest Decade	90's	4.8	90's	9.1	90's	15.9	90's	10.5
Difference		1.3		1.1		1.1		1.0
90's variation from average		0.5		0.7		0.5		0.5

The 90's were the warmest decade for every season. The strongest warming v the century average was in the spring. Winter showed the largest change between the coldest decade and the 90's. Apart from the 90's, the summers of the 30's and 40's were the warmest, with the decadal average being only 0.16°c below the 90's.

Looking at the absolute difference between the winters and summers, the most "continental " decade was the 40's,with a range of 11.7°c, compared to an average of 10.8°c.

WEATHER EYE COMPETITION

Well done to Karen Wheatley of Dorking who is the Winner of Issue 11's competition. She received a copy of the Natural History of Selborne by Gilbert White and free entry to the museum plus tea for two. She answered correctly `The Bible' to the question, ' What is the World's most published book'? Many thanks to all readers who took part. Runner Up is Mr Derek Thomas of Portchester who wins a signed Hampshire and Isle of Wight Weather Book.

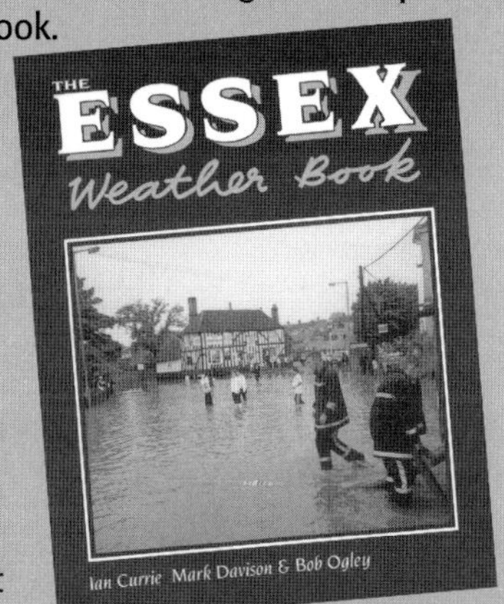

Issue 12's competition is a copy of the Essex Weather Book. To win this 168 page exciting signed book, recently updated, with over 160 dramatic photographs answer the following question: What were the 3 terrible UK Weather disasters in the first year of our present Queen's reign? Send it to Weather eye, 77 Rickman Hill Coulsdon, Surrey CR5 3DT with your name and address. Expiry date: 31st May 2003.

There will be three other prizes including `Weather of the 90s' by Peter Wright and Robert Fitzroy's 1860 Barometer Manual.

MARCH 'MANY WEATHERS' 1965

by Tudor Hughes

To most people the month of March means the end of winter or at least its worst manifestations. Not only is it warmer but it is so much lighter. There is an old weather saying, "as the days grow longer the cold grows stronger". It is appropriate as although by March the sun can really have an effect and March days are 3 to 4 degrees warmer than those in January at night there is much less difference and March frosts are quite common.

High pressure can often give some cold but sunny days in winter as here at Kings College, Cambridge in late January 1965. Picture Norman Brooks.

FOURPENCE (by po

FRIDAY, MARCH 5, 1965

★ THE LONG, LONG TRAIL ★

"It's quicker on foot!" Certainly, the young lady in our photograph at Brighton-road, Coulsdon, seemed to be proving the point yesterday (Thursday) when winter returned with a vengeance and a queue of traffic, which held up public transport, stretched from Hooley to Croydon—and well beyond.

SUDDEN SNOWFALL CAUSES CHAOS ON THE ROADS

Traffic held up for miles: Trains forced to emergency working

THE sudden snow-fall yesterday (Thursday) reduced traffic conditions to what was described in some quarters as 'the worst-ever'. On all the main roads there were solid lines of traffic, trains were as much as two hours late, and buses in certain parts stopped running.

Lines of crawling traffic stretched from Hooley as far as the borders of London to ...

motorists who left their cars at home.

British Railways had spray trains out in the Southern Region treating the live rails, and electrically heated points were switched on to prevent them freezing but they were forced to abandon time tables by 9.0 and resort to emergency working.

As was expected such notorious places as Sanderstead-hill, Tithe Pit Shaw-lane, Warlingham, and Church-hill, Caterham, became, for a time, almost impassable. Many cars were ...

trains which should have arrived at local stations at around 8.30 drew in at 9.30.

In Caterham by nine o'clock six inches of snow had fallen, and people were asking themselves: "Is this the start of another arctic winter like the one which started on Boxing Day, 1962, and went on until March 1963?"

Kenley Police had all available men out on the streets, but they were fighting a losing battle and confined their activities to sorting out the worst of the pile-ups and jams.

But even while the work was ...

'TRAFFIC WARDENS' PLAN CRITICS

STRONG opposition was registered by several members at the meeting of Caterham and Warlingham Council to the proposed appointment of traffic wardens in Caterham Valley (reported last week), and the waiting restrictions being placed on cars and other vehicles in certain parts of the valley areas.

In regard to the traffic warden scheme, it was pointed out by Coun. W. D. Gearing, and the Highways Committee chairman, Coun. A Morris, that this was a police appointment, and had nothing to do with the council, although the Highways Committee supported the idea.

Members were also reminded ...

Caterham Times - March 5th 1965

Because of this greater strength of the sun the range of temperature during March can be quite spectacular, none more so than in the March of 1965. The month started with cold north-easterly winds and some snow but on the night of the 2nd/3rd the sky cleared and the temperature over much of southern England fell to -10°C, which is cold for midwinter, let alone March. At Corwen in North Wales the mercury sank to minus 21.7C[-7F]. An area of low pressure then moved southeastwards into the continent and overnight heavy snow fell so that on the morning of the 4th there was a level depth of about 6 inches and 9 inches [23cm] in Wiltshire and Hampshire. The temperature that day stayed just below freezing. This was true midwinter weather but it didn't last long as the pressure rose and the days became sunny and eventually quite warm, the temperature on the 13th reaching no less than 15°C, which is not too bad for early May, never mind March. But there was still frost at night every day up to the 11th.

The weather then became unsettled and rather wet for nearly a fortnight. With all the cloud, rain and wind there was no frost but it was very dull, and from the 15th to the 21st there was only 2 hours of sunshine at Bracknell in Berkshire, out of a possible 80 hours. This was all due to low-pressure areas near or to the west of the British Isles, but on the 27th the weather machine suddenly decided we deserved something better and a remarkable change took place. An anticyclone, or area of high pressure developed to the south, moved up over Britain and took residence for several days.

For nearly a week there was barely a cloud in the sky, there were light breezes, the air was very dry and we had a spring heatwave. On the 29th the temperature reached the remarkable figure of 24°C over large areas of inland southern and central England. This, let it be noted, is warmer than the average midsummer day, which touches 21° to 22°C typically. At Wakefield in Yorkshire the mercury reached 25C, a British record for March. On the coast it was much cooler and Brighton on the same day shivered in a very chilly 8°C [46F]. But a remarkable thing happened to the night temperatures, at least inland, because they were now lower than during the previous unsettled spell. There was ground frost widely from the 28th to the 31st and on the 29th, the warmest day of the spell, many places recorded an air frost before the sun got to work. At Bracknell the temperature rose from freezing to 24°C [75F] before dropping back again to 2°C the following night. Winter to summer in nine hours!

This most agreeable weather was caused by an anticyclone and it is interesting to look into why these areas of high pressure usually give good weather, but sometimes not. Anticyclones are formed by a complicated dynamical process in the upper atmosphere which causes the air to slowly descend. As it does so it becomes compressed and warmed. This air can be extremely dry and so is usually cloud-free. The descending air does not normally reach the ground but stops at typically 900 metres [3000 feet] and below that (especially in winter) there may be a layer of cold air. This situation is called a temperature inversion because normally the temperature falls with increasing height. Just below the inversion there is often a layer of cloud and in winter the sun is too weak to disperse it with the result that we get cold, gloomy weather. Or the cloud may dissolve allowing fog to form which again, the sun is often too weak to dispel. The great London smog of 1952 was an extreme example of this, with all the fog and soot being trapped in a cold, dense but shallow layer below the inversion, and with no wind to stir it up. But at any time from mid-March to mid-October the sun has enough strength to dissipate any cloud or fog and actually get through and heat the ground, which in turn heats the air. Above the temperature inversion we already have relatively warm dry air so the sun only has to heat a quite shallow layer with the result that it warms up very quickly. If the lower layer of air is moist then clouds can form but they do not usually amount to much, being suppressed by the dry air above.

It is persistent high pressure that gives us our best summers but why this happens, with one anticyclone after another, is a much more difficult question to answer, as it involves the circulation of the entire Northern Hemisphere, and the oceans as well.

March 2003 was very anticyclonic and some large diurnal ranges of temperature were recorded. For instance at Altnahara [Highland] a minimum of minus 8.6C was followed by a maximum of 16.8C on the 19th, a range of 25.4C [46F]. On the 23rd the Chipstead Valley, Surrey recorded a minimum of minus 5.1C and a maximum of 19.6C, a range of 24.7C. For details of the Chipstead Valley see issue 6.

WEYMOUTH BEATS THE RECORD FOR JANUARY SUN.

Until this year the record amount of January sunshine for anywhere in the UK stood at 115.5 hours at Bournemouth in 1959. January 2003 produced a new record just along the coast at Weymouth, also in Dorset, with 121 hours 48 minutes. This is not far short of averaging 4 hours per day, very impressive for a mid winter month. February 2003 proved to be the sunniest February on record for Scotland.

BALLOONING - AN EXPERIENCE

BY JOHN BIRD.

Fourteen people assembled with some apprehension in a field near Petworth, in Sussex, to take part in a hot air balloon trip as part of a friend of mine's 60th birthday celebrations. The weather was of course the dominant factor as to whether the trip would take place at all. The last week in June in the south east of England had been kind to us all. Even the Wimbledon Tennis Championships had not been interrupted by rain. However, towards the end of that week signs were less optimistic. On the morning of the flight the BBC Weather Centre's observations for the nearest weather station to Petworth as printed out from the internet showed:-

Saturday, 29th June 2002 as at 10.00 hrs Temperature - 16 degrees cent; R.H - 73%; Pressure - 1023mb falling; Vis - excellent and Wind Speed which is very much the key factor - 11 m.p.h. South west. Estimated time of departure was 19.00 hrs but because of a slight deterioration in conditions and the forecast of rising winds and falling pressure decision on take off was delayed until 12.00 hrs. With a large party originating from High Wycombe, Sawbridgeworth (Herts), Epsom and Haslemere abandonment would mean gloom all round and hastily cancelled travelling arrangements. At 13.00 hrs a message was received, however, which gave the go ahead. At 18.30 hrs therefore our group looked apprehensively as passenger baskets, balloon fabrics and burners were unloaded from four wheel drive trucks that arrived at the take off area. One of the balloon team filled a small helium filled toylike balloon and let it go to check the wind strength and direction. All of us were then employed in laying out the main canopy and cold air was blown inside it first of all whilst we were bidden to climb into the compartmentalised basket which lay on its side and for us to hang on to the safety rope handles therein. After a long blast of flame from independent external blowers hot air was belched into the by now half inflated envelope and things developed rapidly with our basket righting itself - much to the relief of the passengers. Save for the fact that the basket was still tethered to a Land Rover it would have left the ground. Upon release from the Land Rover "anchor" however that's what did happen. Being comparatively akin to a convective thermal the whole contraption rose rapidly. The take off site was well chosen with a thick copse of trees on rising ground to the SW (windward) of launch site. Obviously a calm spot is chosen for launch as an awkward wind at that stage could upset plans quite dramatically. Upwards, then, we shot quite rapidly so that within a few seconds we were quickly rewarded with a superb view of the area. Visibility was not what I would have called "excellent". In fact it was "good" at about 15 miles with the South Downs just in view to our starboard quarter as we headed east. Clad in a multi-layered pullover and anorak the temperature at 2000ft seemed little different from that at ground level especially as warmth from the balloon hot air burner was only a few feet away. All those who had been worrying about their vertigo were pleasantly surprised, even though this does affect certain individuals when looking down a steep mountainside. It should not be a deterrent to those contemplating trips of their own. Our pilot was concerned that a south-westerly wind might take us towards Gatwick airport - not to be recommended for balloons. A near miss from an HS 146, a Boeing 737 or the like could soon take the shine off the sport. Thus his intention would have been to land well before we strayed into dangerous airspace. However the wind was kind to us for it turned out to be westerly, not south westerly, thus allowing us to see Gatwick in the distance but well away on our port quarter. Ballooning occurs either early in the morning before convection disturbs the normally calm state of the atmosphere or later in the evening when the sun ceases its diurnal activity and winds die down again Hence one of the reasons why an 18.30hrs flight was approved. However this particular flight was not to conform weather wise. Instead of a wind at 11mph as indicated by earlier observations by the end of the flight we had travelled 21 miles in 1 hour and seven minutes which calculated out to about 19 mph. The pilot seemed quite pleased with himself saying this was the longest flight he had performed but that reluctantly he felt he had better close down the operation as by this point we had already strayed east of the main A23 Brighton Road. There were a few caustic comments overheard on the pilots two-way radio coming from the Mini vans chasing us below. They indicated enough mileage had been covered already and they would have to retrace more miles than they had planned to get us back to base before nightfall - and our dinner which was to be held back for us at the local pub in Northchapel! Priority was then given by our Captain to a study of the area for a good landing. It might be surprising for readers to know that, even with the environmental call to save our trees suggesting a dearth of them in this particular area the land was extremely well wooded. However, given the need to give power lines, railways and main roads a wide berth, our man suddenly indicated that "there's a lovely bit of set aside down there" and immediately headed for it with expert precision. Thus, the time had come for the pilot to issue commands to passengers as to how to keep their heads down and hold on for a landing. Now landing at 12 mph would have been good news but a landing speed of 19/20 mph was rather daunting. The first touch with land would create a bump he said and that there would be a second bump probably heavier than the first. Thus, with every confidence in our Captain and a hurried wave to a family enjoying an evening's siesta beside their swimming pool not far below us the first bump seemed a long time coming as we held tightly on to the safety ropes inside the basket. Our safety "tutorial" by our man at the helm proved to be very correct. Our first bump left us still upright but with a deflating envelope the second bump with terra firma turned the basket and ourselves into horizontal mode and continuing in that position we scraped through the grasses as we slowed to a stop. As the certificate issued to balloonists at the end of the flight said rather poetically," on this day as the holder ascended into the sky in a hot air balloon he became at one with the wind". Not quite what a meteorologist would say but a statement of some meaning I suppose to the romantics in this life. As a prologue to this event it can be said that the weather was in a deteriorating state and balloon trips were not "the flavour" of the next week or so. On the day of the trip barometric pres-sure was 1023mb but each day after that a continual procession of depressions crossed Britain. Over a 12-day period approx. 60 mm of rain fell. Our increasing wind on the evening of the flight at a time of day when conditions should have been calming down was therefore a precursor to this wet period.

Waiting for lift off. Picture provided by John Bird.

THE RAGING FIRES OF CANBERRA

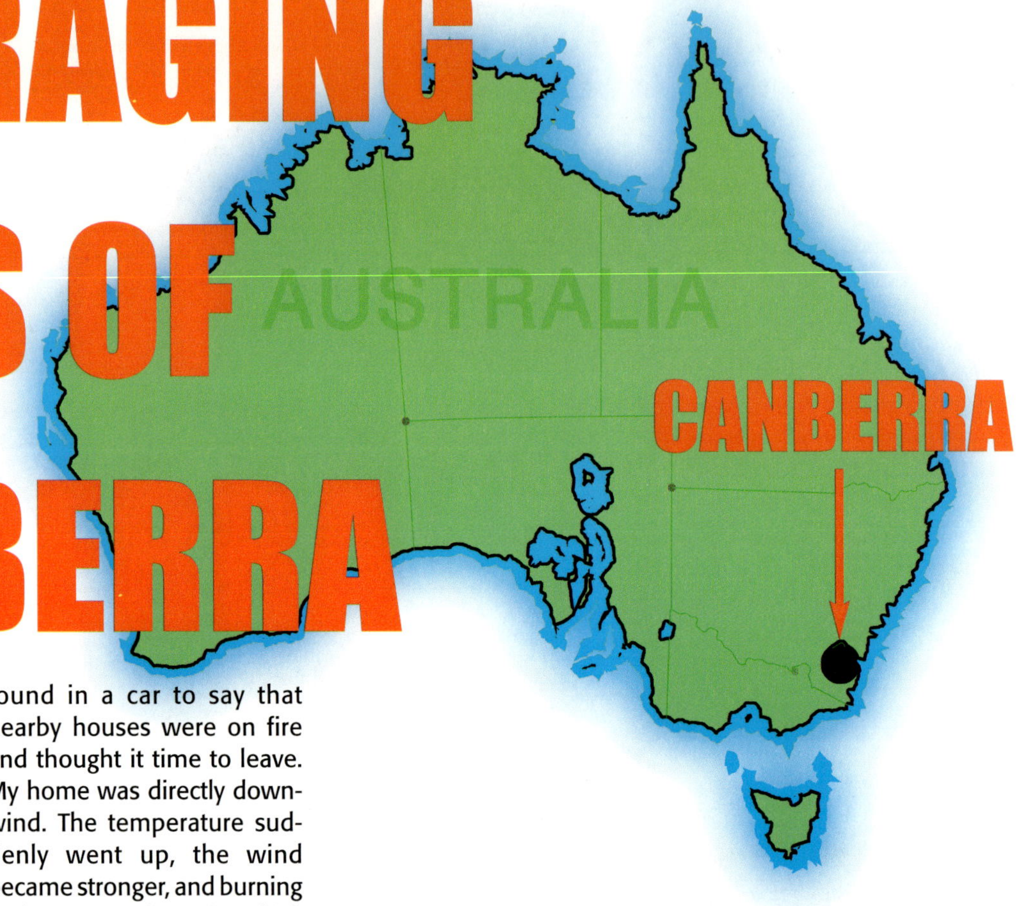

Mr Raven of West Wickham in Kent kindly sent this account to me. He received it on the 20th January 2003 from his nephew living in Canberra, Australia. The fires had made World News.

Ian, my brother was staying for the Weekend, and we had gone to see an Exhibition on the Saturday morning. Upon leaving the event the sky was dark with smoke. We visited friends in a nearby suburb, and while there the sky grew darker still- a nasty grey-black purple with overtones of sickly yellow. The wireless was advising people in the suburb of Duffy [and others] to return home. So we did.There was a strong north-west wind blowing, so the whole of the western flank of the city was exposed to fires. The temperature was about 38C at about 3.30 PM, and it was so dark that the sensor lights kept on switching on and off. We prepared rubbish bins of water, and had wet towels to swing at spot fires that result from burning embers that land at random ahead of the front. I also loaded up my housemates car [he actually lives some-where else, but I look after his car] with photographs and a few personal items ready to leave if we had to. And then someone from the other end of Derwent Street came round in a car to say that nearby houses were on fire and thought it time to leave. My home was directly downwind. The temperature suddenly went up, the wind became stronger, and burning embers started coming thick and fast. I have some idea of how quick fire can travel in such conditions, and know that under these circumstances, if the fire front arrived-wet towels and hoses are hopeless. We both left, drove to a car park and remained in the car for about 45 minutes, until the wind died away. We then returned home fearing the worst but the house and surrounds were OK. Ian and I carried on wetting the garden and house into the night. The electricity was off for the next 24 hours, but was switched on last night. My emergency was over. Ian returned to Katoomba last night on the train. It was not the Weekend he was expecting, but one we'll both remember for a long time. It was reassuring to have him around at the time. Tragically 4 people were killed, more than 350 homes were lost and the Mount Stromio Observatory was totally destroyed. The city will rebuild and life return to `normal' but Canberra won't forget what happened on the 18th January 2003.

BERLIN'S AIRBORNE FLOOD PREVENTION SCHEME.

Graeme Stockton took this interesting picture. This is what he says: - The large airborne, and ugly, pipes interested me in the Kju'damm, Berlin's Oxford Street. So I took a photograph and asked what they were. Berlin is apparently very swampy and where new buildings are being built a network of pipes drain the land into the nearest canal. It struck me as a similar exercise to that undertaken in Chichester during the Floods of 2000/01 [See issue 7]. The practical solution appears to override the pleasing look in this Germany City. I cannot imagine this in London's Regent Street.

CIGARS AND PLATES LENTICULAR CLOUDS.

AS SEEN ON THE FRONT COVER

This excellent cloud picture has been sent to Weather eye from Mr Jeremy Early. It was taken in the Yellowstone National Park, Wyoming, USA, above the Madison River. It is a good example of a lenticular cloud. These are lens or cigar shaped clouds that develop when a humid layer of air is sandwiched between dry stable layers as it crosses hills or mountains. These clouds though can also form a long way downstream of high ground. They are often very smooth outlined and can persist in situ for some considerable time. The clouds are of the type altocumulus and are medium level cloud which in the British Isles means between about 2000-6000 metres in height [6500 feet to 20,000 feet].

When there are multiple layers they take the form of `piles d'assiettes' or `pile of plates cloud'. These clouds have sometimes been mis-taken for flying saucers. Occasionally lenticular clouds can be etched by a beautiful iridescence of reds and greens, sometimes blue and yellow. They are caused by diffraction or bending of light rays by very small tightly packed super cooled water droplets that make up the cloud.

We are very grateful to Mrs Simone Thornton of Walton-on-Thames for this striking picture. It is shows a type of cirrus called vertebratus which has the appearance of ribs or vertebrae. Cirrus is a high level ice cloud in this case above 9000 metres or 30,000 feet.

ISSUE 11

Weather eYe

In search of the Brocken Spectre

The Horsham Storm

Gilbert White's Weather World.

Terror in Poole Harbour

Weather eYe

"For everybody fascinated by the Weather."

Published by: Frosted Earth, 77 Rickman Hill, Coulsdon, Surrey CR5 3DT

Printed by: Litho Techniques Ltd, 46-50 Godstone Road, Whyteleafe, Surrey CR3 0EA

From the Editor

Once again many thanks to those subscribers, who provided articles, pictures and even a poem for this issue. I would also like to credit Andrea Richichi for the Yakutsk pictures used on page 8 in the previous issue 10. I hope to produce even better issues of Weather eye in 2003. If you have any ideas for articles or questions about the Weather please contact me at Weather eye. Why not give the first 10 issues of Weather eye to a friend or relative as a present this Christmas. Sent in an attractive plastic wallet it makes an appealing and informative gift for a special price of just £10 and to complete the offer I would give the next two issues as an extra too. Or there is a signed copy of the Hampshire and Isle of Wight Weather Book available for just £7 including postage and packing. Other offers are on the Frosted Earth web site. Don't forget the Weather Eye Competition on page 11. Enough of the commercials may I take this opportunity of wishing everyone a cloud nine Christmas and a sunny New Year.

Best wishes - Ian Currie

FRONT COVER: *Thunderstorm over the Harz National Park, Germany, August 2002.*

INSIDE FRONT COVER: The World's largest Weather House, authenticated by the Guinness Book of Records, at Gernrode, Germany.

A LOSS ADJUSTER'S VIEW of the weather part 2..

by Malcolm Johnson

One might be forgiven for thinking that a property claims handler has little to worry him from the weather viewpoint during a hot dry summer, but nothing could be further from the truth.

With doors and windows left open for air, there is a great temptation for thieves to get in and steal property, whilst the temperature in the roof space can rise to a very high level. This can result in plastic water supply pipes springing apart at the joints causing water to cascade down through the house.

I can recall dealing with such an escape of water claim following hot weather on 24 August 2001, when the temperature reached 32°C. The owner of the house returned from holiday to find the interior of the property on both floors saturated. Ceilings had been brought down and carpets, bedding and clothing sodden. He had left a key with his neighbour who, on seeing water pouring out of the front door was able to get in and turn off the water supply, but by then the damage had been done. The insured was faced with a need to find alternative accommodation, whilst I arranged for a damage management specialist to restore the power supply and install dehumidifiers to dry the place out. Virtually all of the contents had been damaged beyond restoration and had to be replaced and major building and decorating work undertaken which, as the house had only been built four months earlier and almost everything was brand new, proved soul destroying.

It was Charles 2nd who described the English summer as comprising "three fine days and a thunderstorm" and indeed there is some truth in this. On 4 July 2001, following three warm, sunny days a severe thunderstorm occurred close to my home at Havant, Hampshire, striking the cross on the roof of St Michael and All Saints Roman Catholic Church and setting the church alight along with the adjacent Priests House. Such claims are, mercifully, rare but electrical systems and apparatus are frequently damaged in such incidents, resulting in insurance companies having to meet the cost of repair or replacement.

Summer heat can also cause other, more unexpected problems as I found out in August 1990. On 3 August at Hamworthy, Dorset a nurse came home from work in the early afternoon and opened the patio door to the lounge, which faced south. She received a shock when the double glazed door fell out of its track and landed on the patio, breaking the outer pane of glass. She submitted a claim for the damage to her insurers and, as she could not explain why it had happened, they instructed me to visit and try to find the answer. The door was of 'upvc' construction and I recalled that the day on which the incident occurred was the hottest of the century in many places, with the temperature reaching 36°C in the area and 37.2°C in Cheltenham, Gloucestershire. I noticed that the door track was distorted and it was clear that this had been caused by the heat, so that when the door was pulled it had simply come loose and fallen out.

The most common problem for insurers in long periods of hot weather occurs in areas which have a shrinkable clay subsoil, particularly if properties have large trees nearby. The drying out of the soil, exacerbated by the leeching of moisture by tree roots can cause the foundations of the house to subside.

Such problems tend to manifest themselves in September and early October and the movement can on occasions be sudden and dramatic. I can recall visiting one such house in 1989 in North London, accompanied by the property owner's surveyor who had attended for the first time a couple of days earlier. At my meeting he handed me a copy of his report detailing the damage and we walked around together checking that it was accurate. In almost every room the cracks in the walls were wider than he had noted and there were more of them, but the greatest shock to him occurred when we went into the back garden to look at the rear elevation. He had just told me that it was unaffected and there was no need to inspect it, but I insisted we did so ,"just to make sure". It was just as well that we did, for there were cracks nearly one inch in width and we had to make urgent arrangements for the rear of the house to be shored up. This was all rather different from the recommendation in his report to "keep an eye on the cracks which should hopefully close during the winter as rainfall rehydrates the subsoil"! There was a large tree growing in the back garden which had clearly made the problem more dramatic than it usually is, for generally the surveyor's initial recommendation would have been correct. Crack repairs and redecoration would have been the only work necessary after removal of the tree and monitoring of the damage. In this case, however, despite removing the tree a scheme of underpinning of the foundations had to be carried out to stabilize the property, followed by crack repairs and redecoration.

You can see from these cases that the weather in summer can create many and varied problems for insurers, perhaps even more so than in winter.

August 1995 was the warmest on record. This pond at Purley Oaks, South Croydon, completly dried up.

Beauty and tranquillity at Sheffield Park Garden, East Sussex, during October 2001. This month was the warmest on record in the C.E.T. Series back to 1659. Picture by Joan Spershott.

Hoar-Frost in Shropshire, 31st December 2001. Picture by Mike Mildren.

Above & Below: Hoar-Frost built up like snow over several days in South Croydon at the beginning of January 2002. Pictures by Eddie Whiston.

Somerset House Ice Rink, during December 2001. The last real Frost Fair in central London was in February 1814. For 1000 years of great winters read Frost, Freezes and Fairs, by Ian Currie.

THE HORSHAM STORM

FRIDAY 5TH SEPTEMBER 1958

Tudor Hughes

It is not often one witnesses a truly momentous piece of weather and, for many, this is probably a good thing, given that extreme weather can cause damage and even loss of life. But the violent thunderstorm that occurred early on Friday evening, 5 September 1958 caused no deaths (except drowned livestock) though there was much local flooding and considerable hail damage. To this writer, as a carefree 15-year-old, it was simply a great spectacle, which has barely been repeated in the 44 years since.

After a rather poor summer, the weather became warm in early September 1958, and by the 5th it was distinctly hot and humid, with the temperature reaching 25-26°C. Our family had gone for a car ride to Ashdown Forest in Sussex in the afternoon, and on the way back, between 6.30 and 7 pm, the sky grew eerily dark. By the time we reached Caterham, Surrey, the sky was gloomy, sinister and greenish, with lightning flickering continuously. When we arrived home, at 7 o'clock, it went completely black and the heavens opened. About 57mm [2.25 inches] of rain fell in three-quarters of an hour, accompanied by the most spectacular electrical display I have ever seen, with forked lightning, sheet lightning and every other sort of lightning shooting across the sky in all directions. The garden was flooded and a one-foot wall of water shot out into the road on opening the garage door. The rain subsided, but the lightning went on for some time and was of a type I have not seen since, advancing across the sky at a measurable speed instead of an instant flash.

So far I have described only what I saw, but in Horsham, West Sussex, it was rather more serious. Hailstones the size and weight of cricket balls (5oz/140g) fell over parts of the town and in villages to the south such as Southwater, these being the largest ever known in this country, and caused considerable damage. Furthermore, two tornadoes hit the outskirts of the town, twisting large trees off above the ground and destroying a petrol station. At Gatwick Airport a gust of 85mph was recorded and a hangar was wrecked.

Where did this monster come from and what caused it? It seems to have first really got going just west of Chichester in the early afternoon and moved northeastwards, intensifying as it drew in warm air over the land. It was joined by another storm that formed north of Brighton and moved north-northeastwards, the two combining near Knockholt, Kent, where 128mm or 5 inches of rain fell in 3 hours. At Swanley, Kent, 57mm of rain fell in no more than 20 minutes! The storm ploughed on into Essex, where 75mm or 3 inches of rain fell in a number of places.

The storm happened because the air was unstable with a rapid fall of temperature with height. This means that any rising air (which also cools due to expansion) remains warmer than its surroundings and on this day was able to rise to great heights [52,000ft, nearly 15,000 metres] condensing out its moisture as it did so. The updraught in this case was powerful enough to keep cricket-ball-sized hailstones in suspension and must have been at least 80mph. This rapid condensation of large amounts of moisture puts a tremendous amount of water into the cloud, and as soon as it leaves the updraught, it falls to earth in torrents.

It would have taken a very bold weatherman to forecast a storm of this intensity, and to predict the track well nigh impossible. Although the right conditions for thunderstorms existed over a large part of the country a storm only broke out in one place, as often happens. In this case a light easterly breeze met an equally light northerly from a weak high-pressure area to the north-west, the two converging along a zone aligned south-west-northeast. Where these two winds met there was nowhere to go but up, and it is probable that this was the trigger. Because the conditions were favourable, the storm, having started, was self-sustaining for as long as there was a supply of warm moist air for it to draw upon.

SOWING WILD OATS!

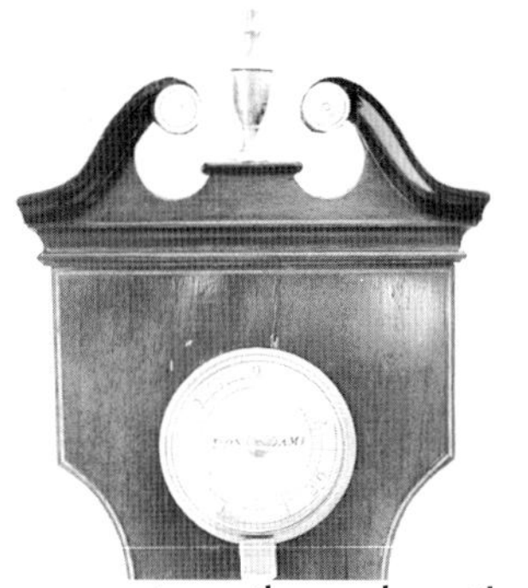

by Philip Collins

I must stress that I do not admit to sowing any wild oats, but my Father does! And they grow to over 6 foot in good soil. Wild oats are without doubt a terrible weed in some areas of the country. Like many things however there is actually a useful aspect to these clever weeds.

Many antique mercurial barometers incorporate a hygrometer; these were actually operated by part of a wild oat. The photograph shows this simple domestic instrument removed from its case. The upright stem which operates it is more commonly called the oatbeard obtained from the wild oat seed. When magnified one can see that its structure is that of a twisted fibre, like that of a rope, and has been used for its natural ability to twist to the right when moistened, and to the left when drying. The rate of movement will vary from oatbeard to oatbeard as they vary slightly in length and thickness. Some turn two or three revolutions when moistened and some will turn even more. This action stands the seed upwards with the aid of the tail, or arm, which is set at right angles to enable the seed therefore to locate a crack or crevice in the soil structure of the ground in which to drop, thereby increasing its chances of propagation.

The use in the hygrometer dials of antique barometers was commonplace up until approximately 1840 when some makers must presumably have tried to cut corners on production costs. Generally barometers not originally fitted with wild oatbeards are of poor quality. This tendency seemed to increase as the years went by, perhaps the start of mass production! And more profit! Although there are fine examples of operational hygrometers with oatbeards after 1840, they seem to be almost non existent after the 1870's. The typical barometer which did not usually have an oatbeard fitted is the 'onion' or 'tulip' design barometer. A cross section of the middle of the hygrometer dial often encountered on such barometers, fig. 2, and of the earlier style, fig. 1 – which actually works (!) – illustrates this progression. When using an oatbeard, some support is needed, even when only slightly encumbered with a dried grass pointer, to enable the pointer to revolve near enough parallel to the dial and not twist up to the glass or down to touch the dial. This is provided by a brass tube surrounding the oatbeard. It is interesting to note that on some early stick barometers circa 1790 and earlier, which are filled with oatbeard hygrometers, the allowance for length of the beard is greater than most normal wheel barometers of later date. It is perhaps possible that in the 18th century larger oatbeards were more commonly available or brought from overseas where in hotter climates they are generally twice as large as today's British varieties. As an experiment wild oats have been grown which have oatbeards of approximately ½" long and operate well when used as described, but accuracy is just not available; the best one can hope for is a comparative indication. The divisions on the dial are almost meaningless. Although few people observe these hygrometers, the only satisfactory course when restoring them is to make it as near the original as possible.

Wild oats were used more in Europe than in the British Isles. Simple little moisture (Hygrometer) gauges can be made by gluing an oat beard to a piece of card and mounting a lightweight pointer on the top. Some older farmers and country people I have spoken to remember playing with the wild oat seeds when children, if you have any further knowledge about this often overlooked weed then please do write to me.

Philip Collins. Barometer World & Museum
Quicksilver Barn, Merton, Devon EX20 3DS.

Curator, Restorer, Maker, Author and specialist in barometers.
Tel:
01805 603443
Fax:
01805 603344,
e-mail:
philip.collins@barometerworld.co.uk

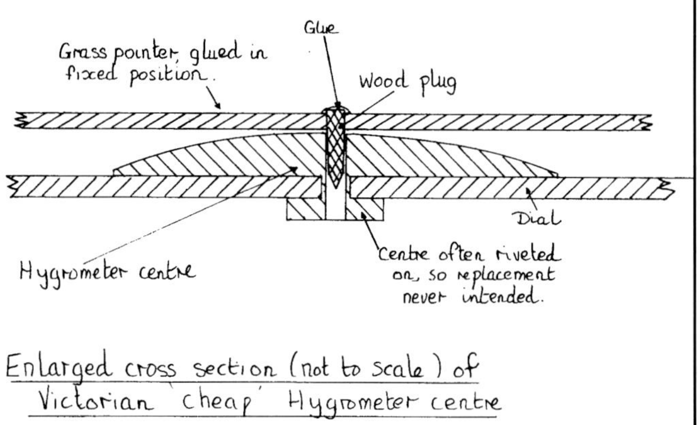

FIG 1

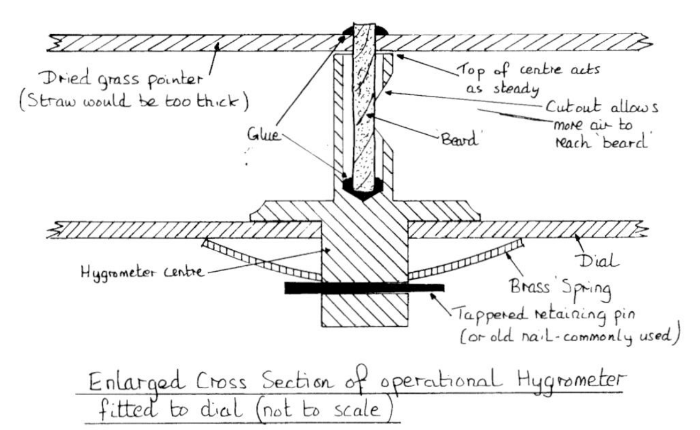

FIG 2

ONE LOW...

...AFTER ANOTHER DECEMBER 1912

In a normal autumn or winter month the west of Britain is wetter than the east but December 1912 was exceptional. Depression after depression tracked across the Atlantic passing northwest of Ireland and Scotland. It resulted in a flow of very moist and boisterous south west winds throughout the month and it was often quite stormy. Prodigious amounts of rain fell in the hills and mountains with Princetown on Dartmoor recording 406mm of rain, Borrowdale in the Lake District 598mm and 756mm fell at Loch Quoich in Invernesshire.

Yet in the rain shadow of the Pennines Thirsk recorded only 23mm and Middlesborough 25mm [1inch].

Some of the wildest weather took place over the Christmas Period when a terrific southwest gale developed. West facing windows were smeared with salt even on the lee side of the Pennines in Durham. On the Isle of Man many roofs were ripped off and windows blown in. Across Scotland a vast amount of timber was blown down and buildings collapsed in Dumfries. Along the south coast there was an exceptional tide especially around the Solent and Southampton Water. Part of the sea wall was swept away at Portchester and flooding washed fruit trees out of the ground from gardens in Milford. The wind averaged storm force 10 along exposed sections of the south coast. An observer at Fareham in Hampshire described Christmas Day as cheerless with the rain falling in sheets.

The Conwy valley of north Wales experienced a great flood when part of a three-mile length of embankment, 6m or 17 foot high, built to keep out the river collapsed. Huge masses of water engulfed the lowlands drowning animals and destroying crops. The wind was so strong that huge waves built up across the vast stretch of water and sent spray high into the air and across the wooded hillside beyond.

It was a difficult time for shipping and the fierce winds forced the 6,500 ton SS *Tripolitania (above)* onto Loe Bar near Helston, Cornwall. Of the crew of 28 men and boys, 27 were saved, one fellow drowned. The vessel remained there for two years despite repeated efforts to refloat it and was eventually broken up where it lay. A local man, Henry Trengrouse, invented a rocket firing device to send a line to a stricken ship after the HMS *Anson* foundered on another occasion in the same place with the loss of over 100 lives.

Gilbert White's weather world

Gilbert White was born on 18th July 1720 in the vicarage of Selborne in Hampshire. The church house lay alongside St Mary's Church where his grandfather was vicar and where his parents were visiting at the time of his birth.

He was 9 when he came to live permanently in Selborne at a house called *The Wakes* located on the other side of the green from the vicarage. He attended school in Basingstoke and thence to Oxford University becoming a Fellow of Oriel College.

By 1747 after obtaining a BA and MA he was made deacon at Christ Church Oxford and accepted a curacy at Swarraton and Bradley. Two years later he was ordained as a priest. In 1751 due to the illness of the vicar at Selborne he became curate in his home village. He never strayed too far being curate at nearby Farringdon for 24 years. The last 9 years of his life he was curate of his home village again. Most of his duties could be carried out from *The Wakes (above)*.

This potted summary of White's life does not seem too inspirational nor enduring yet in 1788 he published "The Natural History and Antiquities of Selborne" and by this one book became one of the most well-known writers in English literature. Subsequently published in over 200 editions [reputedly the 4th most published book in the English language] it made this self effacing man who refused all offers of promotion so as to stay close to his village, a person who is now known throughout the world. People still avidly enjoy the atmosphere and detail of his writings. He kept a record of his gardening activities entitled *The Garden Kalendar* and devised a Naturalist's Journal which included a day by day record of temperature, pressure, wind, rain, weather conditions and phenological information from 1768 almost to his death in 1793.

Gilbert White had a very keen sense of observation of all things natural, including the Weather. Although not a trained scientist he recorded precisely and with scientific method. He discovered the hitherto unidentified smallest British mammal, the harvest mouse and was the first to distinguish between the chiff-chaff, the willow-warbler and the wood-warbler. He kept excellent phenological records [see *Weather eye* issue 6 page 11].

Below are a selection of some of his weather observations.

He mentioned that a true reference to rainfall of an area is when a long period of data is used. He began rainfall readings in *1779* and the total for the year was 28.37 inches whereas in *1782* 50.26 inches was recorded.

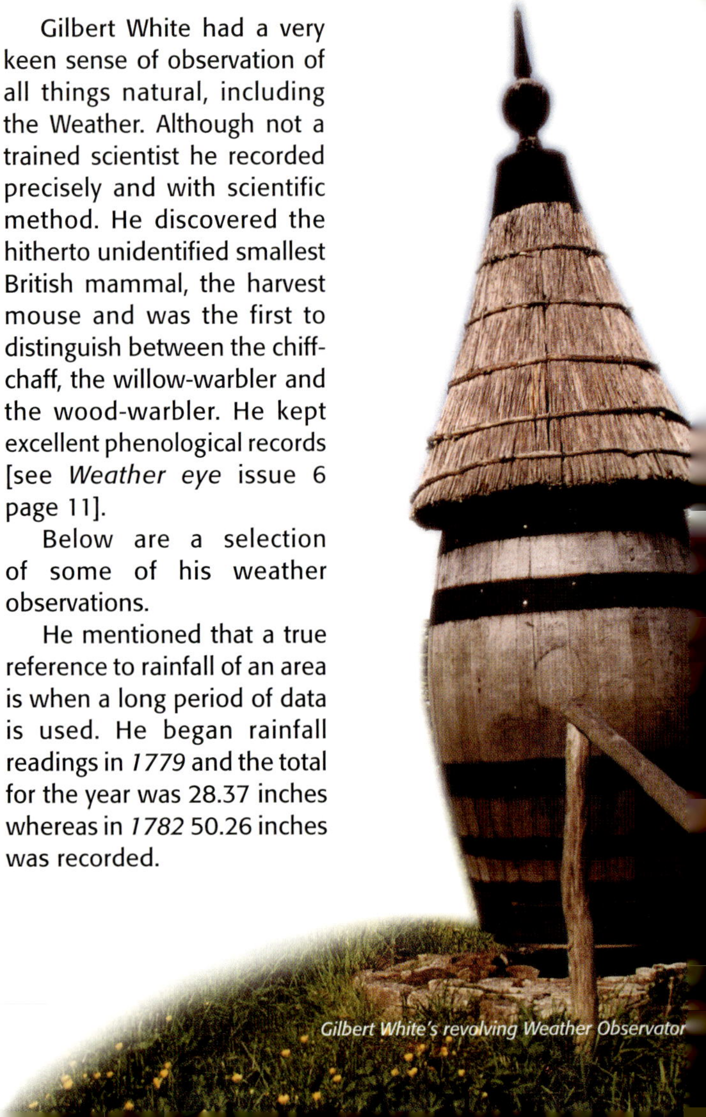

Gilbert White's revolving Weather Observator

In January *1768* there was a severe frost and deep snow. A thermometer measured 14 and half degrees below freezing point within his house. Outside tender evergreens were much injured but he stated that it was lucky that there was a thick snow cover which insulated some plants. It was the worst frost since *1740*. There are various references to the memorable year of 1740 when due to chill winds even through May fieldfares and redwings stayed on until June.

1774 was a very wet year and there was a great landslip close by at Hawkley. See *Weather eye* issue 3 page 10.

Gilbert White mentioned the fact when corresponding with Dr Huxham of Plymouth that Selborne matches or exceeds the former in rainfall. He correctly alludes to the fact that rainfall is enhanced by the hills to the south of Selborne.

He carried out experiments with mercury barometers comparing the level at Selborne with a nearby higher village, Newton Valence and found it was $\frac{3}{10}$ inch lower and that it fell $\frac{1}{10}$ inch for 100 feet. He construed that the height difference between Newton and Selborne was higher than supposed.

January *1776* was very severe and there was prodigious snow with the "works of men totally overwhelmed" and on the 27th the cold was intense and the quicksilver sunk exactly to zero. In December *1787* after another great snowfall he conducted an experiment which showed that Selborne was a "frost hollow". The mercury dropped to −1.5°F but at Newton Valence a similar thermometer set up read 18°F warmer. There was severe frost damage at Selborne but none at Newton. He also describes the appearance of ice needles or prisms falling from a clear sky, that the fur of his cat was electric and two men suffered frostbite.

He spoke of less cold conditions in the north of England and wondered at the way that latitude can be overbalanced

There are some wonderful descriptions of how sublimely beautiful the weather can be when on 21 September *1741* he describes how it was cloudless, calm, serene and worthy of the South of France itself.

In the summers of *1781* and *1783* he alludes to the heat island affect of London and other towns by saying that the mercury only showed 80°F at Selborne but it reached 84°F in the city.

He was interested in fog drip from trees and cited a misty day in October *1775* when an oak in leaf dropped so fast that the court way stood in puddles and the ruts ran with water but away from the tree the ground was dusty. He links this to places in other countries that rely on fog drip for irrigation and mentions somewhat prophetically that cutting down trees can alter climate.

He provides an interesting description of the lurid blood coloured sun that gave a rust-coloured ferruginous light on the ground in July *1783* linked to volcanic eruption of Skaptár-jökull, in Iceland. This month was the warmest July on record prior to 1983 in the Central England Temperature Index.

He described a severe hail and thunderstorm on 5 June *1784* with stones 3 inches in girth and when they fell on ponds caused froth and spray to rise 3 feet into the air. Hail broke windows at The Wakes. A dramatic end to his book.

TERROR

in Poole Harbour, Dorset.

A series of dramatic storms struck the south coast of Dorset, Hampshire and Sussex on the 5th June 1983. They virtually appeared from nowhere as the early morning forecast had been for a fine day. By midday the sky had turned black and there was stygian gloom over Bournemouth and Poole Harbour. Suddenly vicious squalls and golf ball sized hail lashed the area and made it a harrowing experience for yachtsmen. Mr David Bennett managed to photograph the hail from his boat as the ice hit the water sending up plumes of spray.

This same storm gave a remarkable fall of coal and coke in nearby Bournemouth. One lady picked up 92 pieces on her lawn and some were encased in ice. A herd of cattle stampeded after being bombarded by the unusual objects and a lady out in her garden trying to rescue a pet tortoise was badly bruised. Green houses were shattered. The coal and coke was probably picked up by a tornado that passed over an old industrial site west of Wareham.

Large hail falling in Poole Harbour. Photographed by David Bennett, June 5th 1983.

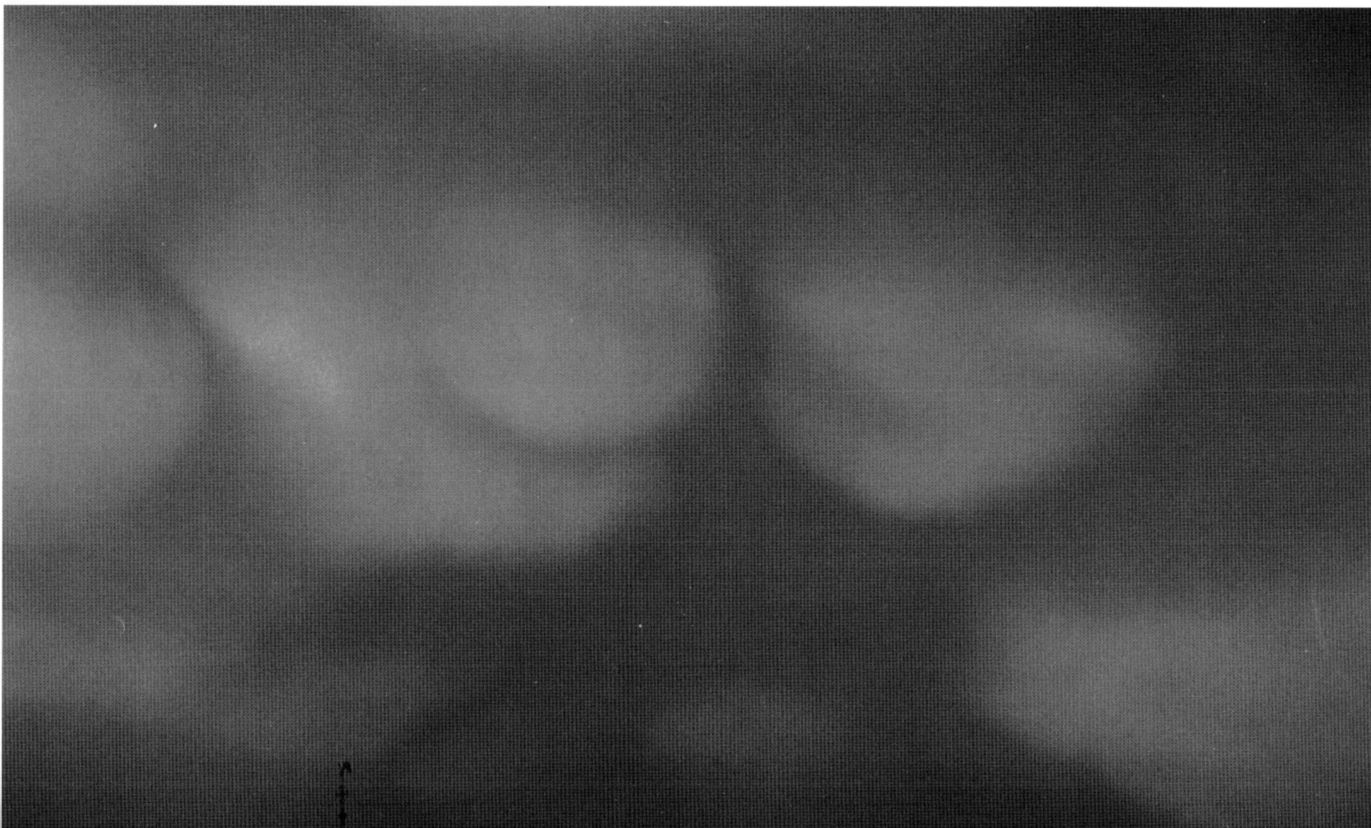

Mammatus cloud *seen here at Dorking in Surrey on the 30th April 2002 by Martin J Clancey. The word comes from the Latin 'mamma' meaning breast and these clouds are pouch shaped or udderlike. They are formed when cold air descends in the rear of the shower cloud. The ice crystals or water droplets in the cloud whilst sinking cool the air beneath which leads to further condensation and down ward protuberances are formed. Also the icy anvil loses heat by radiation from its top. Mamma is best seen when it is underlit by a low sun and can be one of the most spectacular of cloud forms.*

Mamma can form in other cloud. On a day with a moist lower layer fairly near the surface but drier and stable air above cloud will quickly form and then spread outwards unable to rise much into the stable layer. The cloud droplets fall and cool the air below and form pouch like masses in stratocumulus. They can be quite dark in nature due to the bigger droplets absorbing light rather than scattering it and if the sun is rather low in the sky it can look threatening.

In this picture though the descending air was in the rear of a fairly active cold front as it passed through before sunset.

THE FOUR SEASONS

by Heather Jewell

When I wore my Easter bonnet,
Floods of rain fell down upon it.

At my summer barbecue
Half the guests caught winter 'flu.

Autumn wasn't any better
Harvest supper never wetter.

Winter floods of such profusion
Made me come to this conclusion

It must have been an English fella
Who first invented that useful umbrella.

Editor's note: It was Jonas Handway , a Londoner in 1760 who started the fashion of men's umbrellas to ward off rain but it was some 40 years before the idea began to catch on. By the end of the nineteenth century it was an indispensable item.

Weather Eye Competition

Gilbert White's Book `The Natural History of Selborne' is reputedly the 4th most published book in the World. To win a copy of this book, free entry to the Gilbert White Museum at Selborne ,Hampshire, and tea for two after you have looked round answer the following question:

What is the World's most published book. Is it ?

a) The Guinness Book of Records

b) The Bible

c) The Complete works of Shakespeare

d) Harry Potter.

A runner up prize is a signed copy of The Hampshire and Isle of Wight Weather Book by Mark Davison and Ian Currie.

Reply to Weather eye magazine at 77,Rickman Hill, Coulsdon, Surrey, CR5 3DT giving your name, address and/or telephone number.

Closing Date January 31st 2003.

In Search of the Brocken Spectre

Photo by Nik Szymanek courtesy of Les Cowley. See more images and explanations at www.sundog.clara.co.uk

I had been planning for some time to visit the Harz area and climb the Brocken, it's highest peak. It is known for giving its name to the Brocken spectre, an optical phenomenon. I flew into Hannover on 21 July with my family and intended to head straight to the Harz but with the worst flooding for over a 100 years less than 90 miles away I decided to head east to Magdeburg and monitor events on the river Elbe for *Weather eye*.

In fact looking at the map I drove to a town called Schönebeck just to the south of the city and it was a wise choice. Many places were no-go areas with troops and police cordoning off flooded towns and villages all along the river Elbe but Schönebeck had been saved. The Burgermeister hearing of the devastating floods upstream lost no time in contacting colleagues in Cologne on the Rhine and asked if they could advise on flood prevention. They sent special barriers and together with the use of several hundred thousand sandbags managed to keep out much of the floodwater.

The flooding was the result of enormous falls of rain. For instance one location to the south of Dresden upstream from Schönebeck recorded 312mm in 24 hours. Many places in the upper part of the Elbe catchment had over 3 times their August average rainfall in just 12 days and some exceeded 4 times. At 08.00hrs CET on 17 August the water reached an historic high point in Dresden of 9.4 metres beating the previous record of 9.04 metres in March 1845. The average summer flow is 232m^3 but reached over 5,000m^3 during the 2002 floods. Some of the Elbe's tributaries such as the Moldau and Mulde produced massive devastation. The town of Grimma had much of the old part was destroyed. Further upstream the city of Prague in the Czech Republic declared a state of emergency. Sirens wailed across the city and over 40,000 people were evacuated from their homes. Some 8 per cent of the city was inundated with half the underground system out of action.

The cause of the rainfall was a convergence zone where warm moist air from the warmer than average Mediterranean sea was lifted by cooler air from Biscay where the sea was below par in temperature. The effect was enhanced orographically by the hills south of Dresden. In spite of the record high river levels preliminary research by the Meteorological Department at the University of Leipzig suggests that there is no evidence to suggest there is a pattern of increased summer river levels.

During my visit to the Harz I stayed at Gernrode and imagine my surprise on arrival to find that the village boasts two world weather related records. Firstly it is the site of the largest Weather house [see issue 10], which is quite literally the size of a dwelling and secondly has the world's tallest wooden thermometer that also stands as tall as a house. Both have approval from the *Guinness Book of Records*.

The Harz is a so-called Mittelgebirge, a low mountain range, 180km long and 30km wide. The highest peak is the Brocken, 1,142m a.s.l., a granite and gneiss massive. According to German legend it was here that a witches' Sabbath took

The special barriers and liberal use of sandbags saved the town of Schönebeck.

Shown here: Dramatic flood pictures and stories dominated the German Media for much of August 2002.

place every year on the eve of May Day-Walpurgisnacht. Strange happenings of a different kind can sometimes be seen from the summit and I was hoping to witness it known as the Brocken Spectre. It is a ghostly shadow cast on to mist below the observer and can loom large and at a distance. Sometimes a series of coloured rings is seen around the head of the observer with violet on the inside and red on the outside and is called a glory. Light rays being bent or diffracted around the droplets cause the effects.

On my ascent of the Brocken the clouds were well above the summit with no chance of seeing any optical affects but I did observe a marked change of vegetation on the climb. The path I took from the village of Schierke began in towering coniferous forest, which gradually diminish in height and after several scrambles over fields of boulders ends in subalpine heathland. The climate on top of the Brocken is extreme and can be compared to that of northern Iceland. On average there are 300 foggy days a year and the mean annual temperature is 2.6°C. The

The River Elbe became a vast concourse of water, engulfing huge stretches of countryside and cutting road and rail communications. Schönebeck 21st Aug 2002.

result is that the trees do not grow above an elevation of 1,100m. The non-wooded summit is therefore a natural phenomenon.

From 1895 there has been a weather station on the peak and a new observation tower was completed in 1939. The highest annual mean temperature at the summit is 4.8°C in 1989 and the lowest 1.2°C in both 1902 and 1922. Top temperature is 27.9°C on 9 August 1992 and the lowest –28.4°C on 1 February 1956. Precipitation has ranged from the driest year, 1953 with 948mm and the wettest, 2,335mm, in 1981. The Brocken boasts the first cloud chemistry station in Europe as the steep slopes on all sides make the summit plateau almost in a free atmosphere environment. Stratocumulus is the dominant cloud making up 37 per cent of the time when cloud is on the crest. Cumulonimbus makes up 2.1 per cent.

Since the opening of the East German border up to 50,000 people a day make the journey to the peak and there is an important conservation programme to keep visitors to paths and not to trample the unique flora. Even the less energetic can reach the top by steam train built as long ago as 1899.

In 1736 the first shelter for wanderers was constructed called the Wolkenhäuschen or cloud house. A hotel was established since 1908 and 225,000 people came to the summit every year. Between 1961 and 1989 the mountain was part of a prohibited area with the peak bristling with electronic surveillance equipment monitoring the West. Today the building that housed an electronic warfare post of the former East German State security service is now the Brocken Museum. It has a dome-shaped roof and is therefore often referred to as the "mosque". It is packed full of information about the 21,700 hectares of Harz National Park.

A SHROUD OF CLOUD ON THE SOUTH DOWNS

These two picture were taken by Joe Watts, looking south from Plumpton Race Course, East Sussex on Tuesday 23rd April, 2002. Above picture shows moist air spreading in from the English Channel and cloaking the Downs in stratus cloud which cascaded down the scarp slope like a waterfall. It dissipated before reaching the Race Course. Below, the same scene cloud free a few days later.

Sunset over England viewed from Boulogne, France, October 2000. Picture by Dave Stephens, printer of this magazine.

After a very wet, windy and cool day on the 9th August 2002 a clearance to the west in the sheet of altocumulus with some fractostratus below allows some fleeting sunshine just before sunset at Millook Cove, Cornwall. The unsettled weather was caused by a low-pressure system which moved east across southern England and the next day gave severe floods in the Southend area of Essex.

Weather eYe

ISSUE 10

the ISLE OF MAN storm

YAKUTSK A 60 DEGREE BELOW CITY

PLUS

RAIN GAUGE SURVIVES VOLCANO • THE FIRST ITV WEATHERMAN • ROBERT FITZROY

and much more...

Weather eye

"For everybody fascinated by the Weather."

From the Editor

Weather eye has now reached double figures in number of issues. I think it has evolved into an interesting read for Weather devotees. There is still much I would like to offer such as organising weather trips perhaps even abroad, insert more pages, articles, have extra issues per annum and run introductory courses to the World of Weather.

I have been very pleased with the response of readers. You have provided articles, ideas, photographs, suggestions- it all helps to make a pleasing read.

All magazine editors would like more subscribers and Weather eye is no exception. In our case it is to preserve the liberal use of colour and good quality paper, important in making the best reproduction and capturing that weather mood. More subscribers will help to cushion the not inconsiderable expense incurred with each issue and enable Frosted Earth to provide more for you. So if you can continue to recommend Weather eye to friends and acquaintances it will help the magazine to grow from strength to strength.

Please feel free to contact me at Frosted Earth for further details including advertising rates. Back copies are available at a reduced cost to subscribers.

Best wishes for the rest of 2002.

Ian Currie

FRONT COVER: *This sunset picture shows Spring Park between West Wickham, Kent and Croydon, Surrey in February 2001.Following exceptional autumn and winter rainfall the local water table rose to the surface and flooded football, rugby and cricket pitches. The newly formed lake became a haven for aquatic birds and remained until June.*

(This picture will be forthcoming in the Weather Eye postcard set.)

INSIDE FRONT COVER: Seawater surges into Ramsey shopping centre after the storm of Feb 1st 2002. Picture by Luke Edgell CPC.

Published by: Frosted Earth, 77 Rickman Hill, Coulsdon, Surrey CR5 3DT

Printed by: Litho Techniques Ltd, 46-50 Godstone Road Whyteleafe, Surrey CR3 0EA

the ISLE OF MAN storm: 1 february 2002

Mark Davison

Huge seas at the Summerland end of Douglas Promenade, 1st February 2002. Photo Courtesy of Island Photographic.

Residents on the Isle of Man say that the great gale of 1 February was the worst they could remember in the past 25 years.

Millions of pounds worth of damage occurred when a storm surge, caused by a deep area of low pressure down to 928mb in sea area Rockall, combined with storm force winds and a tide three feet higher than had been predicted.

The Isle of Man stands in the Irish Sea, three hours by ferry from Lancashire. Islanders are used to stormy weather but this winter storm took them all by surprise. The Meteorological Office at Ronaldsway said gusts of up to 70mph added around one metre to the high tide. A spokesman said: "With the movement of the earth and moon being so regular, the patterns of the tides are worked out years in advance. The extent of the movement varies through the month between the big 'spring' tide and the small 'neap' tide.

"However, in calculating the height of the water, certain assumptions are made – most significantly that there is no wind and that atmospheric pressure is average.

"Very high pressure can make the sea level lower than it should be and very low pressure can make it higher. Also, strong winds with a long fetch over open water build up a swell which also adds to the height of the sea.

"Big tides happen every month and gales and surges are common during the winter and usually cause inconvenience. If all three factors happen at the same time though, serious problems can occur."

The sea broke through defences at Ramsey and flowed into the town's shopping centre, an extremely rare event.

Dozens of cars were left floating in sea water at the Tongue of Douglas, and tonnes of debris littered the streets at Laxey.

About 50 metres of the parapet wall at Castletown was demolished. Croft seafood factory was partly wrecked by the gale and the Ramsey swing bridge was out of action after water swamped electrical equipment.

The harbour office at Laxey had its roof ripped off and tarmac was ripped up from both Laxey's and Castletown's boat parks.

About 78,000 people live on the island and owing to the its remote location, and being at the mercy of the elements, many islanders are keen weather observers and listen avidly to the shipping forecasts when planning their daily lives.

Speaking at the end of March, Mary Davison, 80, of Mooragh Promenade, Ramsey, said the back of her house was still protected by sandbags after the February storm, and much clearing up was still taking place in the area.

Our thanks to the *Isle of Man Examiner* for their assistance with this article.

Douglas Promenade at the height of the February 1st storm. Photo The Picture Box.

A LOSS ADJUSTER'S VIEW OF THE WEATHER

Malcolm Johnson

The River Wey burst its banks at Guildford after 50mm of rain fell in 24 hours over much of the catchment. This picture was taken on the 7th November 2000.

At 9.00pm on Saturday 28 October 2000, my wife and I sat down to a fish and chip supper, following our return from the CAMRA beer festival at Poole, when the telephone rang. It was one of the Directors of the loss adjusting company I was working for informing me that there had been a tornado at Bognor that afteroon and that they would like me to be on standby to handle any emergency visits that might be required the following day.

In the event my services were not required, but having studied the news and weather reports as well as listening to the weather data broadcast on London VOLMET SOUTH detailing winds gusting in excess of 50 knots it was clear during Sunday afternoon and evening that our office was going to be very busy on the Monday. Indeed, radio reports, on my way to the office, mentioned winds gusting to 67 knots, well in excess of the minimum speed criterion for a storm in insurance terms, with further tornadoes at Selsey and Hayling Island.

We were bombarded with instructions from insurance companies and I headed to Bognor to deal with three of the claims arising from the tornado that had occurred on the Saturday. One of the claims was in Linden Road, part of which was still sealed off by the police. The house I visited had lost extensive areas of tiling to the front and back roof pitches whilst the rear garden had been devastated. It was not, however, as bad as some of the neighbouring properties, one of which had lost an area of its brick gable whilst at another the chimneys had come down.

The next property that I visited had also lost some tiling, guttering and part of its glass conservatory and I met the builder whom the insured had telephoned after the incident. He had made the property safe and we discussed and agreed the costs for repairs before I headed to the third property, which was in Fish Lane just north of the sea front. This was also a bungalow and had sustained damage to both roof slopes as well as the conservatory, garage and brick boundary walls to the rear garden. Rainwater had also penetrated internally affecting the loft and the ceilings, and furniture and carpets in the front and rear reception rooms. Having examined the damage I instructed one of our approved builders to carry out repairs and also asked a restoration company to dry out the interior. The insured was able to stay with his son and family while the repairs were undertaken.

It was clear from listening to BBC Southern Counties Radio that as a result of the very heavy rain that had fallen over the weekend (around 60mm), there was serious flooding in and around Woking and Guildford, which also fell within our branch area, with many properties affected. I therefore agreed to help out and indeed it was that area which was to keep me fully occupied until Christmas.

The first two claims were at Woodstreet Village, just west of Guildford, where rainwater had poured off a farmers field and flooded two chalet bungalows. At the first, the occupants had had a "lie-in" on 30 October and it was their daughter who, having dropped her children at the nearby school and intending to pop in for a cup of coffee, found the road and the front garden of her parents property flooded. The water, which was very muddy, had poured through the bungalow flooding it to a depth of around 15cm and damaging virtually everything within. The situation was made worse as the policyholder's wife was disabled and their buildings insurance policy had not been renewed when it had expired the previous week. I was able to instruct a firm of specialist cleaning contractors to remove any items that were restorable and to thoroughly clean the property and then went next door.

Here the damage was not so bad, partly because the front garden was at a higher level and also because the occupants had got up early for work and had seen the water seeping under the front door. They were able to move large quantities of their personal possessions up to the first floor before things rapidly deteriorated, so that their claim was nothing like as extensive as their neighbours.

From here I headed to Peasmarsh, where the Wey Navigation had burst its banks and flooded a number of properties. The water had entered initially through the airbricks that provide ventilation to the sub-floor void, but had then come in via the lounge doors to flood most of the ground floor. The occupants had only moved in a few weeks earlier and were concerned that the situation could repeat itself in future. Accordingly, whilst repairs were in hand they had arranged, at their expense, for a sump pump assembly to be installed along with an emergency generator to power it.

The scenes of devastation that I encountered on these claims were to be repeated many times over during the next few weeks and for virtually everyone it was a situation they had not encountered before and hopefully would not do so again for a long while. I did however encounter a few properties in Woking and Guildford where the occupants had witnessed the severe flooding which had occurred in Surrey on l5 September 1968 and which had resulted in even greater damage.

While my colleagues and I were able to recommend to insurers that they dealt with the vast majority of claims there were some policyholders who were not so fortunate. For instance where water had entered through basements, insurers were unable to meet the cost of tanking the walls as the properties had either no tanking at the time of the flooding so that the work would be classed as an improvement or it was inadequate. Some of the roofs that were damaged were life expired when the storm hit so that a contribution towards the cost of renewal was all that could be agreed. Whilst in another case the excessive rainfall over the winter period caused a reinforced concrete lintel to deteriorate and collapse again not covered as it was not due to a specific weather event.

The weather events of the 2000/01 winter which I have briefly touched upon provided my colleagues and myself with considerable challenges in dealing with confined and distressed victims of the events and agreeing the ways and means of getting their lives back to normal as quickly as possible. I also found it fascinating to see at first hand the effects of those severe weather events.

Wholesale destruction at Reigate in Surrey after the October 1987 storm and a busy time for loss adjusters. Photo Courtesy of The Surrey Mirror and The Surrey Hurricane Book.

The First ITV Weatherman

by Ian Currie

Laurie West complete with carnation and cheeky smile beside his own innovative weather map.

Imagine my surprise when having given a talk to Hadleigh WI, a lady said that she was going to see a good friend of hers in a week or two, a London weatherman that I might know. I had said previously that I began my weather observations in the London Borough of Greenwich. Even before she had uttered his name I had exclaimed " Laurie West"!

I remember with fascination and delight our first television in 1959. There was Laurie West giving the weather forecast and through my childhood I hardly missed a broadcast of his. Whether it was thick fog, gales or snowstorms he was always swathed in a cheery smile with a flower in his lapel.

Laurie West instructed air crews in meteorology during his RAF days but by the time he retired from the service in 1955 he was an ideal candidate as Associated Rediffusion's TV Weatherman. He was the first independent television forecaster and first full time weatherman as those on the BBC, starting with George Cowling in January 1954, were Met. Office employees and the broadcasts were simply an extension to their daily routine.

Right from the start Laurie spoke in direct terms and appealed to the housewife who wanted to know when it was going to rain rather than knowing it was the result of an occlusion moving slowly east. He even went out amongst the public doing his own market research. By the mid 1960s he had clocked up 2,860 broadcasts to audiences of over 2 million yet still had time to answer a letter I wrote to him aged 12, inquiring about the formation of thunderstorms.

Initially Laurie had to go to Wembley to broadcast and this meant a journey in the underground carrying his rolled up paper map. He then invented his own weather map. It was in the form of three sided metallic extrusions working on a capstan rack turned by hand. Small mobile symbols employed magnets to adhere to it. All this in 1961 before the BBC's use of a seemingly advanced system which included black dots, triangles, and black and white circles introduced by Bert Foorde. Laurie also introduced two weather girls into his programme in 1958 viz. Sheila Matthews and Muriel Young predating the BBC's

The owl which always preceeded Laurie's Forecast.

Barbara Edwards by 16 years. He was also the first celebrity weatherman for he appeared on the Dickie Henderson Show and ITV's UFO. Laurie's main regret was that he only covered the London area and elsewhere it would be the BBC on screen with Jack Armstrong, Downie Armour, TH Clifton and Phillip Allen taking turns to present.

Laurie's last broadcast was in Sept.1968. Thames Television took over and they wanted a new look station with no weathermen though he did a regular Weather slot on the Eamonn Andrews's Friday evening magazine "Today" during 1969.

Now 40 years later I was able to personally thank Laurie for his inspiration and for answering my letter all those years ago. I was invited to spend the afternoon with him in his Sussex home and on the mantle piece was the owl, the logo that began his every broadcast before he came on screen. Now aged 94 Laurie is just as cheerful as ever and was willing to draw five correct entries to the Weather eye competition from an appropriate container, a Snowdon pattern rain gauge.

Competition Winners Issue 9

First was Mr Goulding of Middlesborough who wins the barometer.

Second Mr Powell of Hastings who received a copy of Weather of the 90s by Peter Wright

Third Rosemary Bate of Wantage who was sent a copy of Looking at Weather by Ingrid Holford.

Fourth Mr Yorke of Shaftesbury also sent Looking at the Weather

Fifth was Mr Waygood of Cambridge who received I Spy Weather

Congratulations to all five winners with the answer to the barometer question being Russia or Siberia [though strictly not a country], the Soviet Union or Russian Federation.

There is a new competition this issue, a word search, see page 17 aimed especially for subscribers' children.

Laurie West now aged 94 kindly drawing out the winner of the first Weather Eye competition.

An Observer's Memories 60 years ago

Those who come here to this place so drear
Might just as well be in the Drink.
All the rain on Salisbury Plain
Falls here, or so we think.
I first wrote this verse, it is rather terse
When I was a WAAF Meteorologist.
At RAF Stations we made observations
In rain, hail, snow, sleet and mist.
I was at Netheravon-with its sister Upavon
Both opened in the Great War.
AS one might guess, the Officer's Mess
Was still labelled"Royal Flying Corps".
We read the Barometer and then the Thermometer
That was outside in the Stevenson Screen.
No Satellite, so cloud amounts, types and height
Were just estimated from what could be seen.
The Wind Vane was checked to tell you direct
From which point the wind was blowing.
North, south, west and east, the last was a beast
Especially if it was snowing.
No gadgets you need to check the wind speed
Just look and feel by the Beaufort Scale.
Two equals light air, it won't ruffle you hair
While nine is a very fierce gale.
All this must be coded and the teleprinter loaded
So each RAF group could transmit its Obs.
To Dunstable they went and from that HQ were sent
To every station's Met. Office.

From these Broadcasts we plotted out charts
Every three hours GMT.
From Shetland in the North to Lands End in the South
No Computers as seen on T.V.
With red and blue crayon the fronts were drawn in
Red warm, blue cold, mauve occlusion combined.
Isobars next, Forecasters got vexed
If charts were not ready as timed.
Near sixty years have passed since Netheravon last
In the Winter of forty- four.
But I remember a lot as you can tell from this jot,
If I tried I might even write more.

Olive M Angless – April 2001

YAKUTSK A 60 DEGREE BELOW CITY

by Tudor Hughes

Sunrise over the mighty Lena river near Yakutsk. Like all other rivers in Siberia, the Lena is frozen solid during all winter and spring. The elevated pipeline in the foreground is for hot and cold water, as well as sanitation. To avoid permafrost, everything is built in thick insulated pipes, kept warm by running hot water. Heat and water are distributed in this way from a central power plant to the whole city. The black line extending diagonally to the background is a line of non-heated garages. Cars are left to freeze there during winter. Cars can be used in winter if they are left in heated garages. When parked outside on the street, the engines are always left on.

We in Britain are fortunate that, although our weather can occasionally be hazardous, it does not really dominate our lives. That is not the case in many parts of the world where extreme changes from one season to the next affect the whole lifestyle of the inhabitants. A good example would be the monsoon of India, but in this article we shall be looking at a place with a very different climate, but spectacular nonetheless.

Yakutsk (pron. ykootsk, with the accent on the second syllable) is a large city (pop. 250,000) in the northeast of Siberian Russia. Its climate is an extreme example of the continental type, with warm summers and unbelievably cold winters. The average temperature in January is −43°C. Few people in this country have ever experienced such a low temperature, let alone a month of it. December and February are only a little less cold! When the temperature is that low you cannot just walk outside with a coat on and hope for the best. Every possible square inch of exposed flesh must be covered.

Thick fur-lined boots, gloves and hat are all necessary to avoid frostbite. When the temperature drops below −50°C, as it often does, even deep breathing becomes painful. Children are not spared these rigours and are only excused school when it goes below −51°C.

There are other unfamiliar consequences of the cold. Despite the summer warmth the average year-round temperature is −11°C and the ground is permanently frozen below a couple of feet in depth. This is called permafrost. It is necessary not to disturb this frozen ground and all buildings have a large gap between the floor and the ground and have the appearance of being on stilts. If this is not done the heat from the inside melts the permafrost and the building slumps and eventually collapses. This has happened to some old houses and they have to be abandoned.

There are consequences for motorists, too. Scraping the frost off a windscreen is nothing compared to the problems you have if you've left your car out overnight, unheated, at −45°C. This author, as a former petroleum chemist, knows just how thick motor oil gets at −20°C, let alone −45°C. Even normal brake fluid is pretty tacky at these temperatures and the rubber of tyres becomes so inflexible that the flat part in contact with the road when parked makes the car bump along horribly for a mile or so, until the tyres warm up.

The cold is made more bearable by the very light winds, a gentle north to northwesterly being typical, but a less pleasant phenomenon is the fog which occurs on over half of all days in winter and can last for a week at a time. Much of it is due to the city itself as a source of water vapour from factories and cars. At these low temperatures the air can only hold a minute amount of moisture and any excess from human sources immediately causes a fog, from which tiny ice crystals ("diamond dust") fall gently to the ground.

Despite the dominating influence of the winter cold and the depressing fogs, there is very little weather "action" in Yakutsk. It is very dry, the annual total being only 213mm [a third that of London], most of which falls as showers or thunderstorms in the summer. The small amount of winter snow eventually accumulates to a depth of about a foot, because it never thaws in winter. Its sudden melting at the end of April produces a couple of weeks of flooding which is usually, but not always, well-catered for.

In addition to the dryness, another positive feature of the climate of Yakutsk is its sunshine. The annual total of 2,294hrs is worthy of the Mediterranean and results in large differences between day and night temperatures, particularly in spring and summer. A normal summer in Yakutsk can only be described as "glorious". It is a succession of dry, sunny days with afternoon temperatures of 25°C to 29°C, interspersed with a cooler day or two with a northerly wind and showers, often thundery. Summer 2001 had two successive weeks when the daily

Permafrost at work! More modern constructions are built on stilts, leaving free air circulation under the building. (See text)

temperature reached 30°C or more and the mercury has peaked at 38°C [100°F]. In June the sun shines for an average of 11½ hours a day. But summer is brief and by the end of August the weather is noticeably cooler. The first snow arrives in early October and there will be a snow cover until the first week in May. The inhabitants must then resign themselves to the prospect of the temperature never exceeding freezing point from mid-October to the end of March, and maybe getting as low as −64°C. But preparations for winter can be made because everyone knows what to expect. Gales, blizzards and ice-storms are almost unheard of. It will be sunny or foggy – and, very, very cold.

Data for Yakutsk.

Latitude 62° 05'N Longitude 129° 45'E.

Altitude 100 metres

	JAN	JULY
Mean maximum temp.°C.	-39	26
Mean minimum temp.°C	-47	12
Extremes High	-8	38
Low	-64	-1
Precipitation (mm)	7	43

Total precipitation	213 mm
Total sunshine	2294 hrs
Days with a snow cover	205
Days with fog	59

THE WORLD'S WEATHER
COMES TO BIRMNGHAM

Weather eye editor Ian Currie visited the Stonebee Environment Simulation Chamber at the Outdoor Show in Birmingham's NEC. It can produce temperatures as high as 55C[131F] or as low as minus 30C[-22F]. The former value is not far off the World's highest temperature reading. It can create a light drizzle or a torrential shower, a gentle zephyr or a hurricane. Its principle use is to test travellers' and explorers' clothing and equipment under extreme conditions from polar to jungle environments without them even leaving the country. A thermal imaging camera detects heat loss or gain. Here it is seen with some volunteers braving the cold. Later Stonebee invited me to enter the chamber as well and the weather they provided was a near gale at minus 30C[-22F]. Icicles adorned the walls and frost crunched under foot. Even though Yakutsk is even colder in winter there is very little wind and a value of say minus 40C will be more bearable. Afterwards it felt almost tropical when I sat outside in the Birmingham sun having some lunch with the temperature at 13C[55F].

www.stonebee.com

The Cat and Fiddle pub, between Buxton and Macclesfield.
It is the second highest public house above sea level in England at 1600ft,
This picture was taken at 2.00pm on February 23rd, 2002, by Mark Davison.
The temperature was -1°C and wind averaging at 42 mph in a snow squall.
The wind chill made it feel as cold as Yakutsk.

CLOUDS

Where do they come from and where do they go
The clouds we see in the sky?
Clouds like castles towering high
Telling us rain is nigh.

Small clouds, large clouds, black or white;
Clouds that gather in the night
To bring us rain the following morn
Or harbingers of a rosy dawn.

Fleecy clouds or mackerel skies
Clouds at dusk and at sunrise,
Clouds for ever billowing and blowing
Fast or slow but where are they going?

by Muriel Woolven

The darker patches of cloud are lenticularis, a form of altocumulus, and are formed when a stable layer of air rises over hills or mountains, in this case the North Downs. The cloud is forming on the crests of a train of 'waves'. Aircraft condensation trails are also visible as well as some cirrus fibratus just above the tree

Top left. *Crepuscular rays through gaps in stratocumulus cloud at Horsham in West Sussex. Picture by Sylvia Green. An article on Crepuscular rays can be found in Issue 4 page 14.*
Middle left. *An aircraft has formed a distrail through this band of altocumulus at Pinner, Middlesex. Heat from its exhaust gases has evaporated the supercooled water droplets at this level as well as drier air could well have been entrained downwards from the vortex set up in the wake of the aircraft. On the left to the right of the lamp post is an example of a fall streak hole- see issue 2 page 14.*
Bottom left. *Sometimes during the early evening showers can develop as the breeze dies down and during the day had been too brisk to allow sufficient convection in marginal situations. Quite a heavy shower followed about 20 minutes later.*
Top right. *Altocumulus undulatus top and radiatus below is forming a mackerel sky though it is more often given this name when it is cirrocumulus composed of ice crystals. These clouds are the result of changes of wind speed and direction with height[shear] typical of an approaching depression and fronts.*
Upper right. *Cirrus cloud composed of ice crystals. On right cirrus uncinus [hook shaped],cirrus inortus in middle[tangled] and merging to cirrostratus on left.*
Lower right. *A line of showers developed just to the south of Heathrow airport during mid afternoon, 16th August 2001. One cell had just passed with another following on the same track west to east or right to left in picture. The airport itself remained dry.*
Bottom right. *Stratocumulus arising from the spreading out of cumulus cloud in stable conditions. Taken near Thong in Kent, July 1998.*

rainfall effect on the Pooh Stick Olympics

Under starters orders: the author, 8th owner from left, prepares to launch his spoon into the river Windrush.

To what extent can we hold the weather responsible for observed effects? For instance, the rainfall in a catchment area must affect the current in a river, but what is the delay? And is the current the main factor affecting the speed at which objects float down it? Lets investigate via a charming modern folk custom.

Every Thursday evening in the season, tourists and locals flock to the banks of the Windrush in Bourton-on-the Water (Venice of the Cotswolds) to watch dozens of handmade model boats race 175 metres from the War Memorial bridge to the far end of the village green.

The custom started in 1998 at the Bourton HF (Holiday Fellowship) hotel. Guests stay there to walk the Cotswolds, play golf, bowls or bridge, dance etc. etc. But at the start of each week they are each invited to build a small boat in their spare time, using any materials to hand. Most guests usually join in the fun.

On Thursday, all models are displayed so guests may make a charity donation for the best design. The most popular one wins a small prize for the builder. Then all boats are taken down to the Windrush for the race. At the winning post, marshals in wellies carefully record the winning time and ensure all boats are retrieved. The winner is notionally awarded the Windrush Cup. His/her name is added to a Scroll of Honour for posterity. Other rules (not usually observed in practice) are that the winner shall be addressed as Commodore for the rest of the week, and others should stand when the Commodore enters a room!

In general the better a boat does in the design contest, the more likely it is to sink on the starting line. I simply stuck a plastic spoon through an empty single-portion cream carton. It only earned 50p for charity (from an American lady who thought it was cute) but it came third in the race.

But what interested me was this: can we assume that, from week to week, the fastest boats have uniform performance characteristics? If so, does recent rainfall significantly affect boat speed?

The charts show the results over three summers, with rainfall per month compared to average winning times. It will be seen that the best match is achieved by assuming a two-month delay between rainfall and its effect. Bourton is approx. 12.5kms. from the furthest edge of the catchment area and 160m below it. Is a two-month delay therefore a reasonable assumption? If so, the charts match reasonably well, except for one maverick month each year.

The July 1998 speed is much

too high. But the April rainfall was the highest on record, with floods at Easter. Was this still having an effect?

In July 1999, conversely, the speed is much too low. But May was unusually warm. Did much of the rain evaporate?

In May 2000, the speed is enormously high. But again there was a record April rainfall with a 35% increase from that of April 1998. Was it somehow coming through ahead of schedule?

The race is occasionally held outside the summer season, but not often enough for reliable trends. Speeds are always high off-season, although winters in the Cotswolds have not been noticeably wetter than the summers on many occasions. The fastest speed to date was achieved by Melissa Ridley, on 19th April 2001, with a time of 3 minutes 29 seconds, 50.2 metres per minute. The slowest winner was on 23 September 1998, timed at 8 minutes 47 seconds or 19.9 metres per minute.

Is there any other factor to be considered? Yes – wind direction and speed. When I took part, I carefully chose a central position (see photo) to achieve maximum benefit of the current. Immediately after the launch, I realized my error. There was a barely noticeable breeze from the right, but most boats – even my plastic spoon – were quickly pushed onto the left bank. Thc eventual winner had been craftily (or luckily?) launched from the right-hand bank! Strong winds, from various directions, could clearly produce maverick results at times. Future competitors, take heed!

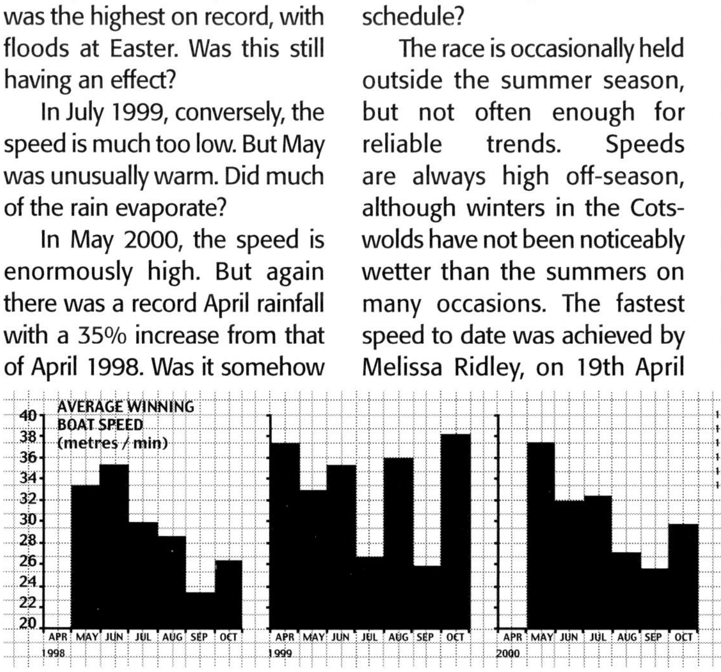

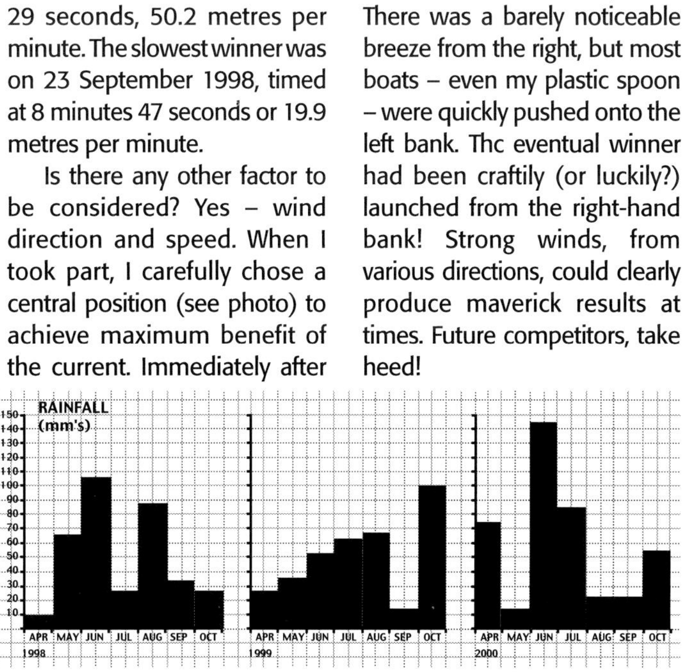

CASELLA INSTRUMENTS IN THE CARIBBEAN MUDFLOWS

Ten British rainfall measuring instruments are currently sited on the Caribbean island of Montserrat as part of a two-year research programme being carried out to discover the relationship between rainfall and the production of volcanic mudflows. They have caused severe disruption since the islands volcano started erupting in 1995.

These flows are generated when heavy rain falls on the loose material continuously generated by the active volcano and so far have helped to bury the islands capital, Plymouth, as well as covering bridges and roads and destroying the island's only golf course.

Now a team, from the University of East Anglia headed by volcanologist Jenni Barclay, is undertaking research with the UK Natural Environment Research Council to ascertain whether or not it will be possible to give prior warning of future mudflows. One of the paths of these flows lies across a route used for daytime entry and prior warning of these flows would help to warn inhabitants when access is more dangerous.

Jenni and her team, also working in collaboration with the Montserrat Volcano Observatory, have positioned ten rainfall recorders from Bedford-based manufacturers of environmental instrumentation Casella CEL in relevant sites at varying distances from the Soufriere Hills. Some are in the islands exclusion zone, which may only be entered with special permission, while others are so remote they can only be reached by helicopter.

Over the next two years the Observatory will be collecting data from the rain gauges on the amount of rainfall and its intensity and forwarding it to the UEA at Norwich for analysis. There the team will examine the information alongside the statistics to be supplied from other equipment located to monitor vibration within the ground.

All the data is then compared with the results of analysis of the deposits undertaken at Norwich.

Dr Barclay comments: "Soufriere Hills has been active since 1995. Like many other volcanoes, it tends to produce a build up in the form of a dome rather than spew out lava on an ongoing basis. Under certain conditions these domes collapse and spill thousands of tons of sticky mud down the sides of the volcano, with catastrophic results in some cases.

"By using instrumentation to provide data we will combine meteorological expertise with a detailed knowledge of volcanoes that will assist us to predict when such events may happen in the future."

To ensure ongoing efficiency of the rain gauges in an atmosphere constantly filled with volcanic ash, the team experimented on the Casella equipment before they left the UK by subjecting it to showers of talcum powder and assessing the amount of ingress that could distort the information it produced.

"As we can make only occasional visits to the locations we needed the assurance that the equipment we were leaving behind would perform. Not only did we receive a substantial amount of advice from Casella, we were also supplied with equipment that we were able to leave on the island with confidence," Jenni added.

The latest update from the university's Dr Adrian Matthews is that the rain gauges are standing up well to everything the volcano is throwing at them. "One was moved 10m bodily on its concrete plinth during a period of volcanic activity, but amazingly it stayed upright and carried on recording," he says. (see back cover)

THE WEATHER HOUSE

Weather eye subscriber Mr Chris Goldie spent some time recently on the Isle of Wight and whilst there his wife bought him a Weather house. He asks what is the history of the Weather house and how do they work?

The device is basically a wooden construction, often modelled on a house, cottage or chalet, that has two doors or windows. At one opening a figure of a lady appears, the other a man according to variations of humidity. The movements are controlled by a piece of cat gut or hair which stretches or shrinks according to the amount of water vapour present in the atmosphere. The house is calibrated so that the women appears when the humidity is low and signifies fine weather.

The instrument is really a hygrometer, a measurer of atmospheric humidity by the method of absorption. In the seventeenth century it was known that certain substances react to changes in atmospheric moisture. Leonardo da Vinci described `a scales' holding a pan of wax and a pan of cotton. Cotton absorbs water whilst the wax did not and the pans tilted as the weight changed. Mizaldus mentions cat gut changing in length as early as1554. In 1664 Robert Hooke said that catgut is not as a good as a beard of wild oat and made a device using it. Others such as Foucher in 1672 used paper, Lana used rope and Saussere in 1780 implemented ordinary human hair and found that it varies by one forty-second part of its length between saturated and dry air. He devised a brass frame with a 7 inch hair calibrated using a scale of 0 to 100 and thus was borne the hair hygrometer readers will know today.

The Weather house came into vogue during the eighteenth century and was well known by 1735 and was often given the term "Dutch Weather house". It has limitations for a damp dewy morning can often presage a fine afternoon. Misty or foggy weather is settled with little rain but registers very humid. In spring showers can break out when the atmosphere at the surface is very dry. A Weather house in a centrally heated dwelling will not register anything but dry!

Two other methods of humidity measurement are by condensation i.e. dew point instruments and by evaporation i.e. wet and dry-bulb thermometers.

TOPIC	ISSUE NUMBER								
April Weather Sayings	1	2							
August Bank Holiday on Ice			3						
Barometers in Devon by Philip Collins				4					
Beachy Head landslip January 1999			3						
Ben Nevis Observatory					5				
Chipstead Valley						6			
Crepuscular Rays				4					
Cumulonimbus Cloud	1								
Davis Index by John Trenchard									9
Dorset's Soggy Secret 1995 Flood by Mark Ching						6			
Easter 1998 Floods		2							
Eclipse 1999 by Mark Davison				4					
Electricty and Climate			3						
Fall Steak Hole		2							
Flavours of Brazil								8	
Floods 1774			3						
Floods Tempests and Future Weather							7		
Friendly Fire by Jack Pope				4					
Frosts, freezes and Fairs		2							
Hampton Tornado				4					
Hastings Weather Station				4					
Helen Young						6			
Hurricanes Bonnie and Danielle 1998		2							
Hailstorms Kent and Essex									9
Landslide Britain								8	
Lewes Avalanche 1836 by Mark Ching									9
Lewes Flood 2000							7		
Magdeburg Spheres Experiment						6			
March Weather			3						
Millennium Floods							7		
Mount Washington			3						
Paris Weather Secret								8	
Phenology						6			
Pinnacles Desert								8	
Rime					5				
Ski Jumping in London			3						
Showers Right Across thenBpard Poem				4					
The Balmy Scilly Isles				4					
Snow on High Ground by Alan Crawley									9
Strange Weather for Rio Gallegos by Tudor Hughes									9
Svalbard					5				
Thermometer of the World									9
Tornadoes	1								
Uckfield Flood 2000 and Uckfield Goes Under							7		
Violent Storm 11 - The 1903 Gale									9
Weather Experiment: making a tornado	1								
Weather Experiment: suspended water		2							
Weather Rocks		2							
Weather Signs	1								
Weather and Thatching	1								
Weather Watcher in a Wild Place		2							
When the Oilskin Froze: KIngsdown Lifeboat Station								8	
Whiteout 1978 Blizzard by Mark Ching					5				
Wing Vanes			3						
'Woolly Fleeces' Weather Saying			3						
1947 Revisited by Gerry Southern					5				

Weather Word Search Competition

Kindely devised by Mrs Carol Pearce

Copy the word search and find the following words:

Calm
Climate
Clouds
Drift
Dry
East
Fog
Frost
Gale
Hail
Meteorology
Lightning
Mist
North
Observations
Pressure
Rain
Shower
Sky
Snow
Snowstorm
South
Storm
Sunshine
Temperature
Thunder
Weather
Wet
West
Wind

Z	A	X	D	W	I	N	D	F	O	L	L	I	A	H
G	A	E	E	E	S	T	M	I	S	T	Y	O	U	Y
M	G	T	R	A	I	N	C	B	S	E	A	S	T	I
I	N	A	T	T	E	M	P	E	R	A	T	U	R	E
S	I	L	L	H	K	T	H	U	N	D	E	R	E	R
U	N	O	R	E	W	T	S	D	U	O	L	C	K	D
N	T	H	U	R	S	S	I	N	C	A	L	M	R	S
S	H	M	E	T	E	O	R	O	L	O	G	Y	G	O
H	G	U	S	R	H	U	D	R	I	F	T	C	K	E
I	I	D	P	T	O	T	E	M	M	R	O	T	S	S
N	L	G	R	V	S	H	A	I	A	N	U	H	T	S
E	B	O	B	S	E	R	V	A	T	I	O	N	S	W
W	N	F	A	N	S	T	O	R	E	Z	R	S	E	O
E	T	S	N	O	W	S	T	O	R	M	L	B	W	O
S	T	R	E	W	O	H	S	X	F	R	O	S	T	A

Fill in your details, photocopy this page and send it off to Frosted Earth to enter it into this issue's competition draw, for a signed copy of I Spy Weather. Shown below.

Name ....

Address ....

....

Tel .... eMail ....

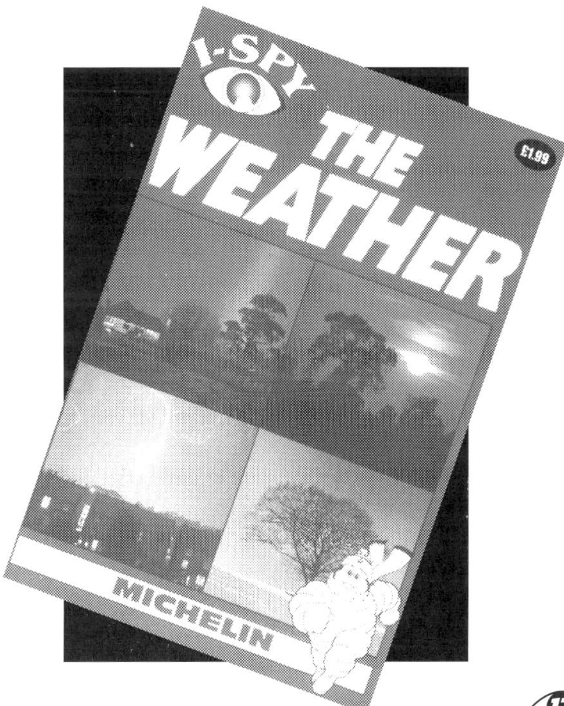

Robert FitzRoy

Founder of the Met Office now a Shipping Area!

by Philip Collins

At the turn of the 19th century, despite the large number of vessels using international trading routes or local, coastal waters there was little meteorological or oceanographic data available. By the middle of the century, however, more interest in the science of meteorology was being taken in Britain and many other industrialised countries.

Improved meteorological understanding offered:

i. Increased profitability of trade due to more efficient usage of shipping. Published charts of prevailing winds and current, meant firm data to plan optimum routes for voyages. (Increased awareness that time was money.)

ii. Prospect of lessening the considerable perils of sea transport through greater knowledge of the nature of storms and consequently improving safety at sea and reducing loss of life.

iii. Possibility of strategic military advantage derived from greater knowledge of storms.

iv. Also, men of science favoured the study of meteorology simply for its own sake.

The creation in Britain of the small, new, government-funded department devoted to the study of meteorology in 1854, paved the way for the professional service that the Meteorological Office provides today.

A senior naval captain, with a distinguished career behind him & high social standing, Robert FitzRoy was appointed Head of the new Meteorological Dept on 1 August 1854.

FitzRoy, renowned for his voyage as Captain of the *Beagle*, the ship that carried naturalist Charles Darwin on a 5-year journey (1831–1836) around South America and up to the Galapagos Islands, had long been convinced of the importance of meteorology to seafaring men and had strong views on the need for weather consciousness amongst ships masters.

Shortly after Fitzroy had assumed command of the *Beagle* in 1829 he almost lost her in a violent storm off the coast of South America. He ascribed the near disaster to a failure in his use of the barometer. The lesson was never forgotten. He became a strong advocate for training ship's officers in a proper understanding of the instrument, and as early as 1843 he outlined a scheme for using barometers to give warning of storms along the coast of Britain.

FitzRoy designed his own barometer, known as Admiral FitzRoy's Storm Barometer and prepared a manual of directions for its use that went into many editions.

A large number of weather observatories were organised by FitzRoy and weather observations from around the country collated. The information was used to construct what he termed "synoptic" charts with which he was able to study weather patterns. The movement of weather as traced on his charts convinced him that it was possible to predict changes at a locality by combining knowledge of a barometer reading from the site with intelligent interpretation of conditions actually occurring at places upstream. Unfortunately, some of his data was weeks out of date by the time it reached him but this weather forecasting technique: considering weather patterns in neighbouring areas in conjunction with changes in air pressure has changed very little to the present day.

Although the Meteorological Department had been set up as an agency for assisting mariners to achieve more efficient use of their vessels primarily a commercial function, FitzRoy was much more impressed by the possibilities of reducing the appalling annual carnage amongst seamen around the British coasts due to the unpredictable nature of the weather. He was a religious man with a deep humanitarian instinct. As early as 1843 whilst an MP, he had made attempts to improve safety at sea by setting up an investigation into

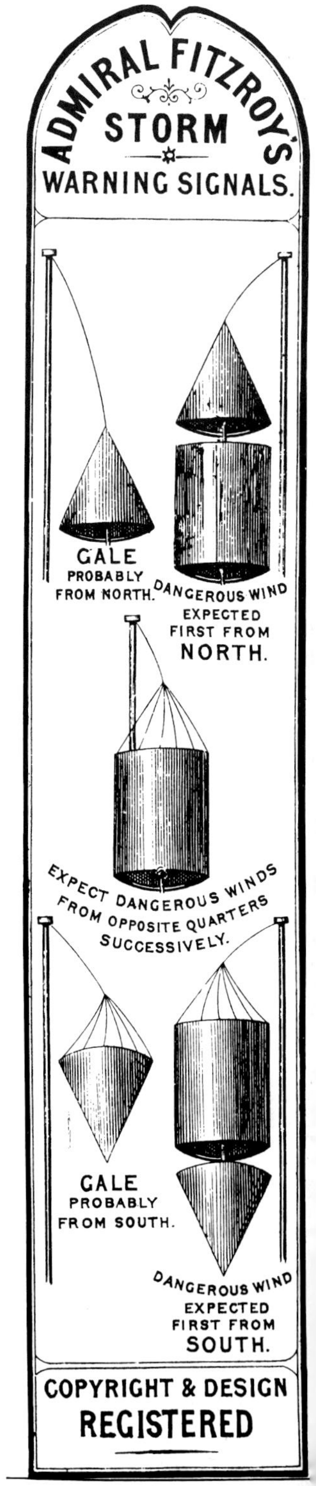

the causes of ship wrecks. In the year when FitzRoy joined the Meteorological Office, in 1854, it is recorded that 1,549 lives were lost at sea. His aim was to provide a full storm warning service for shipping.

By 1857, the Meteorological Department started loaning barometers to fishing villages and other seafaring centres with copies of FitzRoy's Barometer Manual and/or a simplified card containing instructions for using the instrument. This was a very popular service and was extended throughout the country.

In October 1859 the ship The Royal Charter was wrecked on the Angelsey coast in a severe gale with the loss of nearly 500 lives and the steam ship The Great Eastern just narrowly avoided disaster. This convinced Fitzroy that there was an urgent need for storm warnings.

In 1860 FitzRoy used the newly developed electrical telegraph to receive daily observations from coastal stations across the country. A daily exchange with Paris provided a further 6 observations from the continent. Now it was possible to "watch" the rise, force & direction of storms and FitzRoy had the means for sending, in case of sudden danger, a series of storm warnings along the coast. On 6 February 1861, the first storm warnings were issued by telegram to the observation stations likely to be affected.

Simple, visual warning signals were devised by FitzRoy: cones and drums hoisted on a staff outside the observation stations. The Coast Guard and other authorised stations repeated these along the coast when they received a storm warning to inform all mariners of an impending storm, its strength and direction. Despite many attempts, no symbols have been found to improve upon them, the night time equivalent, lights in a triangle or a square are also perfect in their simplicity.

In August 1861 the Meteorological Department started to issue routine weather forecasts and by May 1862, a complete forecasting service was being provided for coastal regions, prepared directly from observations and despatched within an hour.

FitzRoy's labours were cut short by his suicide in 1865. Though much of his work was severely criticized by statisticians after his death, his legacy lives on. Meteorologists today would agree that the modern science is based on many of Robert Fitzroy's principles and despite huge advances in technology, British weather is still extraordinarily difficult to predict accurately!

Above: Robert Fitzroy's grave at All Saints Church, Beulah Hill, Upper Norwood, London.
Right: Admiral Fitzroy Storm Barometer.

Casella's rainfall recorders, fenced off to protect them from wild animals, positioned beneath the active Soufriere Hills volcano on the Caribbean island of Montserrat.

ISSUE 9

Weather eYe

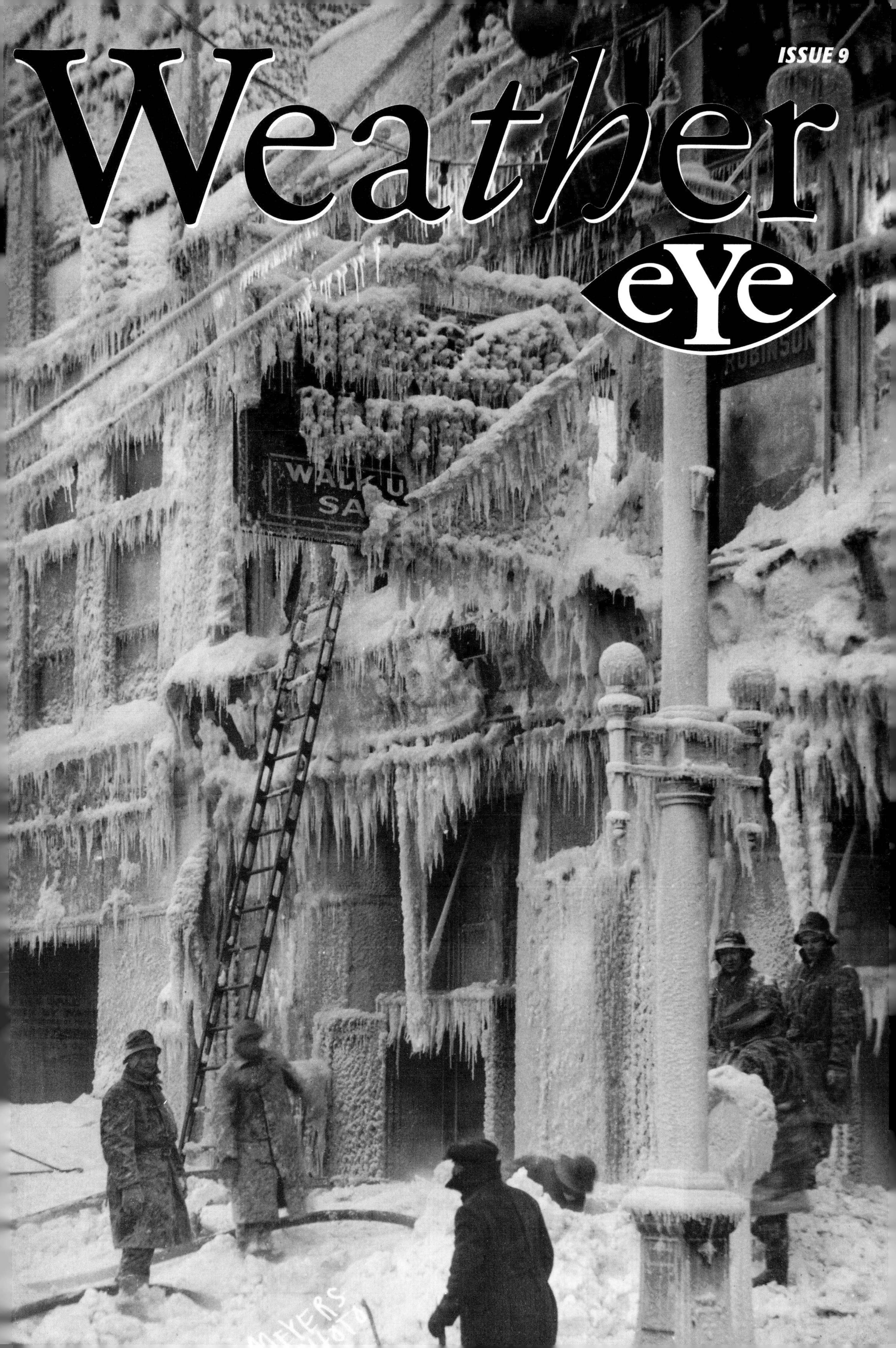

Weather eye

"For everybody fascinated by the Weather."

Inside Cover
Prague in December 1996 with a temperature of -12°c [10F]. The river Vltava is 'steaming'. This phenomenon is called 'arctic sea smoke' or 'steam fog'. It is formed when cold air moves over warm water. Picture by Carole Barlow.

Editor Ian Currie

Subscriptions & back issues to Weather Eye Subscriptions:
77 Rickman Hill, Coulsdon, Surrey CR5 3DT
Tel: 01737 554869 Fax: 01737 554869
Email: iancurrie@frostedearth.com

Front Cover: Water hoses froze almost immediately when firemen tried to put out a fire in Winnipeg, Canada, one January during the early part of the 20th century. The mean maximum temperature is -14°c [7F] and it falls on average to -25°c [-12F].

Back Cover: The A25 Nutfield to Bletchingley road after the great Boxing Day blizzard of 1927. Picture from The Surrey Weather Book

Published by: Frosted Earth, 77 Rickman Hill, Coulsdon, Surrey CR5 3DT

Printed by: Litho Techniques Ltd, 46-50 Godstone Road, Whyteleafe, Surrey CR3 0EA

FROM THE EDITOR

We are now into issue 9 and I am pleased that a number of readers have contributed to this present issue by writing some excellent and varied articles. There are some already in the pipeline for the next issue and I welcome further contributions for inclusion. Photographs, cuttings, cartoons, questions are all helpful. It may not be possible to use every one but I will try my best to include as many as possible. What about a Weather crossword? Issue number 10 will include an index of articles and features.

In this issue Weather eye features for the first time a competition, generously sponsored by Barometer World. All you need to do is answer the easy question and send your reply to Frosted Earth. All winning answers will be put into a draw in March for a top prize of a barometer. There will be several other prizes such as a signed copy of `Weather in the 90s' by Peter Wright, `Looking at the Weather' by Ingrid Holford and titles from Frosted Earth's publications.

May I wish all readers a very pleasant Christmas and best wishes for the New Year. One thing for sure 2002 will provide much weather for us to talk about.

Hail lay like snow at Coggeshall, Essex during the afternoon of Thursday 9th August 2001. Picture by Philippe Hays.

The Kent and Essex Hailstorms, Summer 2001.

By Ian Currie

Hailstones that fell at Horton Kirby, 26th June 2001. Note the two pence piece and walnut for relevance of scale.

Early evening on the 16th July 2001 I was driving along the Darent Valley in west Kent on my way to talk to South Darenth Gardening Club. The venue lay between the villages of South Darenth and Horton Kirby. As I drove along the street I noticed several smashed greenhouses and parked cars had dents on roofs and bonnets.

Arriving at the hall some cars also had indentations and the audience was full of stories of a terrifying hailstorm that had struck the area late in the evening of the 26th June. Remarkably my parents live only two and a half miles to

Damaged car bodywork in the Darent Valley of Kent, as a result of the Hail storm 26th June 2001.

***STOP PRESS!!!** Many parts of East Anglia received over 50mm [2 inches] of rain during the weekend 20th/21st October 2001. Cambridge measured 90mm. There was widespread flooding as shown here at Bocking, Braintree in Essex. Picture by Philippe Hays.*

the west and they were totally ignorant of the event until reading about it in the press though they had been aware of a thunderstorm at the time. The day had been hot and at Northolt [north-west London] the temperature had peaked at 32.2C [90F]. At midday upper air soundings from Herstmonceux in Sussex revealed a reading as high as 6C [43F] at around 3100 metres [10,000 feet]. During the day there was much medium level cloud, a type called floccus, indicating increasing instability. Air pressure was slowly falling as a shallow area of low pressure moved north-east over England and Wales. By 22.00 hrs lightning was flashing to the east of my Surrey station and an hour later the first rumbles of thunder were heard.
Lightning continued to the east for another hour or so but no rain fell.
Meanwhile in the Darent Valley warm air was uplifted to form a huge and cold cumulonimbus cloud. Just before midnight people asleep were awoken by a terrifying clatter. One person described it as "resembling a loud crackling fire" Another person, said she thought her house was going to fall down, the noise was so loud on her roof. The streets were running white with hail, some were almost golf ball sized and penetrated carports, splintered greenhouse glass and dented car bodywork. Flowers were shredded. One nursery in the area had to replace 20 tonnes of glass costing £100,000. Some of the hailstones were gathered up and put in freezers and were given to me to photograph.
As is typical of a hailstorm the path was quite abrupt and less than a mile or so wide running north from Farningham to Dartford along the Darent Valley. Using the TORRO Hailstorm Intensity Scale the storm measured about T4. On a scale 0 to 10 the most severe hail has very rarely reached force 6/7 in this country.
August 9th 2001 was a very different day with a temperature of minus 4C at 3000 metres. A cold pool of air associated with a low-pressure system was moving east across the country. The air at this height was very moist. This triggered a number of thunderstorms giving in places a month's worth of rain. At Northolt [Middlesex] 34mm of rain fell in an hour and 55mm overall with a similar total measured at Ipswich [Suffolk]. Here operations were cancelled at Ipswich Hospital due to a flooded surgery.
Hail fell in places and none more so than at Coggeshall [Essex]. It was not the size of the hail that drew attention but the sheer volume. Accompanied by deafening thunder the hail came down in torrents for 20 minutes, blocking drains and accumulating like a winter snowstorm. Water poured in off the street flooding the Chapel Inn Pub.
Meanwhile at the seaside town of Southwold [Suffolk] holiday makers watched in awe as a waterspout tracked several miles off shore to complete what was a meteorologically very unstable day.

This lovely snow scene was taken near the Tan Hill Inn, northern Pennines, February 1996, by Geoffrey Jacyna.

The Great Lewes Avalanche: Christmas 1836

By Mark Ching

Each winter thousands of skiers and snow boarders make a beeline for Gatwick Airport. It is the departure point for scores of snow-laden destinations across Europe and the USA.

Between Christmas and the middle of April a veritable army of Britons fly away looking for powdery snows and crystal blue skies, all of them hoping to avoid the deadly peril of avalanches that can wreak death and destruction within mountainous areas.

Yet as their flights streak into the Sussex sky little do these snow seekers realise that just below them and but a short drive from Gatwick lies the location of a remarkable avalanche. Never mind the Highlands of Scotland, the Lake District or Snowdonia. None of these more familiar suspects were guilty of playing host on this occasion to one of Nature's most awesome and damaging spectacles.

The tragedy that struck the county town of East Sussex, Lewes, in 1836 is without precedent in lowland Britain. It came less than a month after a severe gale had left a trail of damage across Sussex, coating windows in Lewes with salt blown in from the sea and partly destroying the Brighton Chain Pier.

Christmas Eve arrived in a December that had not been particularly chilly. However the wind had backed to the north-east by the morning and a furious blizzard began and continued more or less unabated throughout the Christmas period. A strong gale blew the enormous volumes of snow into drifts of incredible depths so that all traces of roads were lost and huge barriers of snow prevented all communication between towns.

On its eastern boundary Lewes is guarded by Cliffe Hill, which as the name suggests falls to the edge of the town in a vertiginous perpendicular drop of some 60 metres[200 feet]. Throughout the blizzard the easterly winds roared across the top of the hill and then swirled in great eddies slamming back into the chalk cliff face and plastering it with an ever thickening layer of snow. A monstrous overhanging cornice was formed, a feature well known to hill walkers and mountaineers.

At the foot of the cliff next to Wille's timber yard stood a terrace of cottages called Boulder Row[the name perhaps referring to earlier rock falls]. By the time the storm had blown itself out on Boxing Day the street was overlooked by what was described at the time as "tons and tons of snow hanging in a delicately turned wreath as lightsome as a feather".

This `lightsome wreath' proved a fateful beauty. A sign of the impending disaster was given when a moderate slip destroyed a sawing shed at the timber yard whose owner promptly advised his neighbours to leave without delay. His concern was heightened when an old man recalled that some 50 years beforehand he remembered a similar drift had come crashing down with tremendous violence sweeping all before it into the river Ouse.

However perhaps ignorant of the concept of an avalanche [this was sunny Sussex by the sea after all] most of the occupants of Boulder Row refused to leave. It proved to be a deadly misjudgement.

By mid morning the situation had become increasingly desperate yet the occupants still seemed preoccupied and bewildered by the deadly creation the elements had formed. Mr Robert Hymans who owned the nearby Schooner beer shop rushed into the passageway at the rear of the cottages pleading with the residents to leave. He even tried to drag two women away by force but had to hastily retreat when at that moment the enormous icy cornice gave way and plunged down with brutal force towards the cottages.

The dwellings were struck low and from behind blasting them upwards. Then the avalanche poured over them like a sea, thrusting the houses forwards into the road. Once the snow and dust had settled the view cleared to one of utter devastation. The buildings had vanished.

The immediate aftermath brought men from all over the town to effect a rescue as best they could. There were heart-rending screams from children dispossessed of their parents and mothers frantically searching for their offspring. A young boy called Jeremiah Rook was the first to be dug out. He was alive! Spurred on by this early success the rescuers redoubled their efforts. The next discovery proved somewhat grimmer, a woman found dead, but her final living act had been to protect her child and thanks to her mother's instinct the infant had survived in its snowy tomb. Into the afternoon another four dead bodies were discovered but the recovery of three children alive and well brought cheer to the rescuers. Further snowfalls had encased one of the rescue party up to his neck.

One lad, John Bridgeman, buried for 6 hours, was extracted from the snow after a rafter, pinning him to the ground, had been painstakingly removed.

Although in shock, his leg badly fractured, he thanked his rescuers and called for a drink and was given a glass of beer. Stretchers and blankets were obtained and the dead and injured were brought to a nearby workhouse where several doctors were in attendance.

The final discovery of the day was the dead body of a girl, Susan Hayward, whom John Bridgeman had last seen alive in the passageway behind the cottages.

The subsequent inquest heard that in all 15 people had been buried and 8 had lost their lives. The coroner recorded a verdict of accidental death on the victims and paid a special commendation to the rescuers who had put themselves in grave danger to help their fellow townspeople.

With the exception of Susan Hayward, all those killed were buried in a mass grave at South Malling Churchyard. A marble tablet was placed in the church. The scene of this fatal tragedy is now home to a public house aptly named "The Snowdrop Inn".

A poem describing the episode was published in the Sussex Weekly advertiser in January 1837.

The Avalanche

The snowstorm came on a Christmas night,
And it pil'd its flakes on the cliff's broad height;
And there it lay with fleecy pride,
When the cold sun gleam'd on the mountain's side.
And the cottagers dwelling beneath the hill,
Reckless of danger, regardless of ill
Busied themselves in domestic care,
Mother and daughter and child were there.
The old man close to the fireside stood,
To quicken the course of his torpid blood;
And the budding infant, with its glances sweet,
Gambol'd and crew at the old man's feet.
At length came a sudden rushing sound,
And the avalanche made its fatal bound;
It dealt destruction to all beneath,
And whelm'd the inmates in darkness and death.
Sad and loud was the funeral wail
That was borne abroad on the biting gale;
They gather'd the victims no pow'r could save,
And buried them all in one common grave.
The snow is melted, the storm is past,
And hush'd is the voice of that wintry blast;
Lightly and mild will the summer breeze blow,
And the dead be forgotten who slept in the snow.

The steep cliffs behind the modern Snow Drop Inn, Lewes, were the gathering ground for the enormous amounts of snow that swept through this part of Lewes, Christmas 1836.

THERMOMETER OF THE WORLD

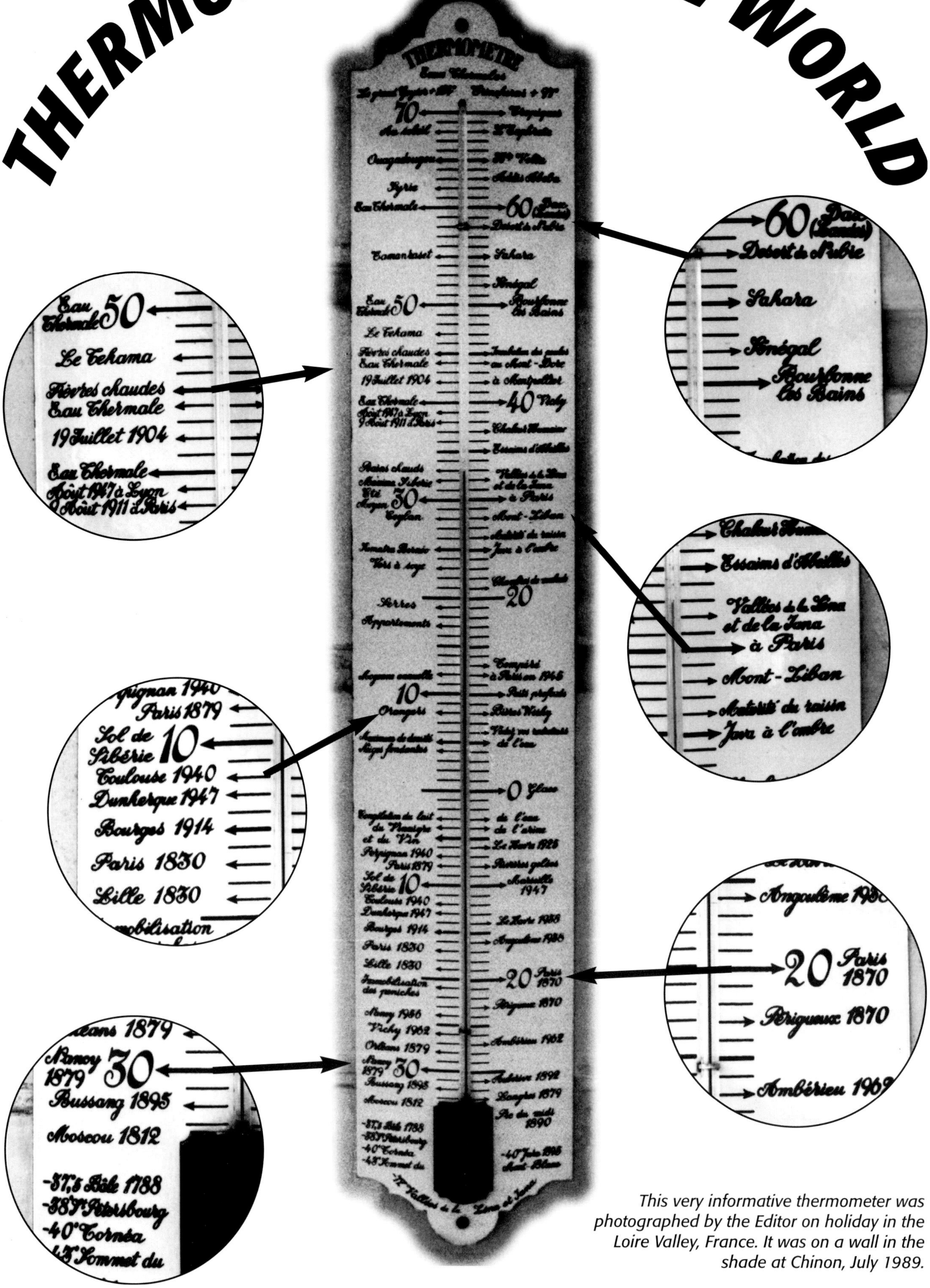

This very informative thermometer was photographed by the Editor on holiday in the Loire Valley, France. It was on a wall in the shade at Chinon, July 1989.

London's Mirror Image? The Strange Weather of Rio Gallegos.

By Tudor Hughes

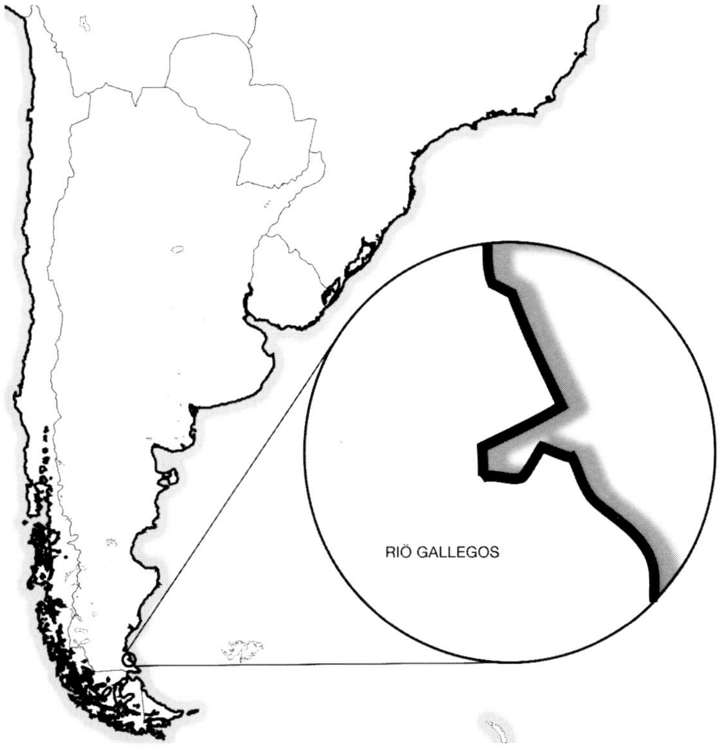

It is interesting to compare the climate of London with cities in similar latitude as they are expected to be alike, being in roughly the same latitude [51°N]. Good examples are Calgary in Canada [very cold in winter], Cologne, Germany, Wroclaw in Poland, and Kiev. These European cities are more comparable to us in climate than Canada, but become increasingly cold in winter as one goes further east.

What about the Southern Hemisphere? The only land at the required latitude [51°S] is the southern tip of South America. There happens to be a town at exactly this latitude, the same distance south of the equator as London is north- the name Río Gallegos. This rather drab workaday town of 90,000 inhabitants, slightly larger than Hastings, is 15 miles inland from the Atlantic coast of Argentina.

How does its climate compare with that of London? It ought to be parallel, not being in the middle of a large continent, and in some ways it is, but there are important differences, that would strike the visitor immediately.

Firstly, it is rather cooler all year round. Frost is frequent in winter though it is hardly of Siberian intensity. Summer days can be quite pleasant, if breezy, with a typical temperature of 18 to 19°C [65F], though the nights are cool.

Secondly, it is windy, disagreeably so, and remarkably, summer is much windier than winter, quite unlike our own weather. Westerly winds prevail with only occasional excursions round to the east, when the weather becomes cloudy and drizzly with air off the cool South Atlantic. The westerlies are surprisingly dry, having crossed the southern Andes. The warmest day last summer [January/February] arrived on a near- gale north-westerly with a temperature of 25°C and 11% relative humidity. In winter the wind exacerbates the cold [typically just above freezing] and a visitor from London used to a westerly wind being mild, would find it all rather nasty. This brings us to the third big difference, which is the dryness.

For a town in the zone of westerly winds Rio Gallegos is remarkably dry. The annual rainfall is just 245mm. Compare this to London with 593 mm or Cardiff with 1065mm. The travel guide mentions clouds of dust blowing everywhere and the airport weather reports sometimes mention "widespread blowing dust", not a familiar feature at Gatwick or Heathrow! Snow is rare though it is often cold enough for it.

The reason for the dryness is the "rain-shadow" effect, whereby most of the moisture in the prevailing westerly winds is dropped on the western slopes of the Andes [which have a tremendous rainfall], leaving the air dry as it descends to the east. Other types of weather such as fog or thunderstorms are quite rare, as they both involve moisture. This climate may not sound too pleasant but it does have the advantage of being fairly sunny. In summer Rio Gallegos records slightly more sun than the sunniest part of England [the south coast] but in winter it has 2-3 times our admittedly meagre ration.

For the more technically-minded, the average barometric pressure is very low especially during the summer when it seems to hover around just below 1000mb. The hot day mentioned above had a reading of 983mb, well into the "wet and stormy" sector on our own barometers. During winter there are more anticyclones and the average pressure is higher, leading to the sunny weather.

Would you want to go there? Well, it is the world's fourth most southerly town but it is 8200 miles away and not a pretty place, although it is a tourist centre for the nearby Argentine Lake District which is said to rival Switzerland.

CLIMATE STATISTICS FOR RIO GALLEGOS

	January	July
Mean Max Temperature °C	18	4
Mean Min Temperature °C	8	-2
Mean air pressure mb	1001	1007
Mean wind speed mph	19	12
Annual rainfall mm	245	
Annual sunshine hours	1950-2000hrs approx.	

CLIMATE STATISTICS FOR LONDON - KEW

	January	July
Mean Max Temperature °C	6	22
Mean Min Temperature °C	2	13
Mean air pressure mb	1016	1017
Mean wind speed mph	7	
Annual rainfall mm	613	
Annual sunshine hours	1568	

Snow on
A mountaineer's lo

by
Alan Crawley

The British mountains cannot always be relied upon to give climbers their beloved snow whenever they want it. I learned this only after a number of frustrating trips to Wales or Scotland in search of ' winter conditions'. Accompanied by my son Jonathan we learnt that just because it was winter on the calendar it need not be winter in the mountains - and sometimes we toiled up the hill sweating in clothing designed for arctic conditions.

The joy of winter mountaineering is its sheer unpredictability. You never know until you set foot on the stuff what the snow will be like. It can be as hard as ice, soft as talcum powder, unstable as sugar or firm as rammed soil. Each has its own hazards and needs to be handled differently.

Early snow was no good for mountaineering. We ruled out November and the first Scottish snowfalls. Even the end of December was still a bit early. Beyond the New Year the days get longer but it can be bitterly cold and the snow can be blown around to form cornices and wind slab. We only climbed in January on three occasions. One was on Dove Crag' s Easy Gully where my son and I walked to the foot of the gully in soft snow. The pitches were covered in loose snow which sheared off under foot. Next day we nearly drowned in spindrift from the previous night's fall. On the whole we preferred to wait until later in the season when it had all settled down. March was our preferred month with April, February and May ranking next in the number of outings on snow. Even in March conditions were mixed with the first half the best. Glencoe is the most popular climbing area in the UK where snow can almost be guaranteed.

Glencoe accidents and rescues are often in the news during winter. For many years it was the home of Hamish Macinnes, local guide and avalanche expert. Nowadays walkers and climbers can check out the likelihood of avalanches on notice boards in valley car parks. Avalanche risk is classified on a scale of 1 [low] to 5 [high].

A typical climb on the mountains of Glencoe took place on the 10th March 1996. Snow lay above 500 metres. We roped up in Coire Nan Lochan and Jonathan, my son, led the first pitch to a rock belay on a ledge. I led over an icy patch and found a small spike of rock in the snow for a running belay but I ran out of rope before I could find any more rock. I buried my deadman in the snow and backed it up with an ice axe belay to bring Jonathan up to the running belay which he tied onto, to allow me to climb on. I reached a snow platform on the left side of the gully and secured myself with my deadman and axe again. Jonathan led through to the top in bright sunshine where we stood and gasped at the brilliant view across Glen Coe to Ben Nevis.

Taking a route up the face of a buttress or along a ridge avoids the risk of being caught in an avalanche in gullies or smoother slopes. There is of course less snow and the ground can be mixed.

Now and then we were very grateful for our windproof clothing which came into its own in strong winds. I had a "montane" suit which has a Pertex outer shell with a fleece lining worn next to the skin and is designed on the principle of` keeping a sheep warm even when it is wet'.

The first winter climb we ever did, East Chockstone Gully, was on a February day in the eastern Lake District. On another occasion, February 25th 1995 my wife Hazel accompanied us. Conditions

Striding Edge, Helvellyn, Lake District, 25th February 1995.

gh Ground
e of the white stuff.

were excellent. On Striding Edge, Helvellyn snow lay under foot above around 600 metres. The skies were blue. It was the sort of day when everyone wore a fixed grin of pleasure on their faces. The final chimney was tricky and I cleared steps for Hazel. After this we put on our crampons. It was a new experience for her and she shot up the snow slopes at a great pace proclaiming the wonders of crampons.

Only in the highest Scottish mountains could we expect to find snow in gullies at the end of May. The north face of Ben Nevis offers such climbs and we had a very enjoyable ascent on the 21st May 1996.

For summer snow the Alps and Pyrenees can still be relied upon but even in our few trips we have seen permanent snow retreating away from the rock leaving unexpected gaps that made some of the old guide book descriptions rather puzzling. Snow on the mountains adds an extra and exciting dimension to mountain climbing. Lets hope that we don't lose this marvellous phenomenon because of climate change.

Glossary.

Belay-*to secure either with a pin or fasten around a rock etc.*

Deadman -*an alloy plate with cable that is buried in the snow to make a fixed belay when there is no rock anchor.*

Crampons- *steel spikes that are strapped underneath each boot to bite into ice or hard snow.*

Easy Gully, Dove Crag, 22nd January 1995.

Alan and Hazel Crawley on Stob Ghabhar looking along the Aonach Eagach ridge, Glencoe, 16th April 2001.

Rain Stopped Play
A look at the Davis Index

By John Trenchard

The happiness of millions and the livelihood of many are irrevocably affected by the prevailing weather conditions and most of us want a fine summer. So how good or bad was that of 2001? There is a method designed to ask just that question. A formula is often used in meteorological circles to enable a valid comparison to be made for a wide number of places in the British Isles. It is based upon the assumption that maximum temperature, sunshine and rainfall are the best elements to use. These elements are weighted so as to make the standard deviation of all three as nearly equal as possible.

The index, known as the Davis index after its inventor is calculated as follows using the months of June, July and August:-

Add ten times the mean daily maximum temperature in degrees Fahrenheit to twenty times the average daily sunshine duration in hours for the period. Then subtract seven times the total rainfall in inches. Thus I= 18T + 20S-7R

Using my readings and daily sunshine amounts for Cardiff Weather Centre published in the daily press, this Davis index for Cardiff becomes 768 for 2001, 785 for 2000 and 771 for 1999.

To make these figures more meaningful we can compare them with Ryde, on the Isle of Wight, where the summer weather pattern is broadly representative of central southern England's coastal resorts during the years 1918 to 1987. The resulting average index is 787. Here is the top 4 :

Year	*Index Score*
1976	915
1949	890
1933	881
1947	871

By contrast the bottom 4 are:-

Year	*Index Score*
1920	695
1954	703
1956	711
1922	717

The approximate value for this summer, 2001, worked out for Hurn near Bournemouth and within sight of the Isle of Wight is 815. "When I was young summers were always fine" is often heard. However if one takes the early 1920s for instance there was great variety. The index measured 695 in 1920, 839 in 1921, 717 in 1922 and 798 in 1923. For younger readers they may recall the summers around 1959, when the index was 719 in 1958, 854 in 1959 and 743 in 1960. This just shows the variable nature of our summers over the decades. Note all these references to this Davis index are for Ryde in the Isle of Wight. However bear in mind that this index is only for June, July and August and takes no account of any good or bad weather in May and September.

On the 19th September I noticed a press report which said that Glamorgan county cricket club had claimed the top spot in the County championship this season - for losing more cricket due to bad weather than any other side in the country. They have been named as the "raining champions", after no fewer than 103.5 hours -that is a quarter of their scheduled championship cricket this summer- was lost to the elements. They pipped Lancashire for this top spot by 3.5 hours. By way of contrast, the Hove-based Sussex have lost the fewest hours, just 27.5 hours, a factor that no doubt will have played a significant part in their promotion to the First Division. Hove had a Davis Index of 826.

Looking at my rainfall records for this summer's cricket season during the period 21st April to 15th September rainfall was only 102% of the long-term average at 422.6mm with a Davis Index of 768.

Editor's note:-
The Davis Index was first published in Weather- a Royal Met.Soc. Publication in August 1968. Mr N E Davis was employed in the Met. Office at Strike Command, High Wycombe. There are several other similar Summer Indices such as 'The Poulter' and 'The Fergusson'.

Huge fires broke out during the long hot summer of 1976. This aerial shot was taken at West Moors, Dorset. 1976 still maintains top spot in the Davis Index. Picture The Dorset Weather Book.

Violent Storm 11. The Great 1903 Gale.

On the 27th Feb. 1903 an intense low-pressure system crossed Ireland and moved north-east over eastern Scotland deepening to 953mb [28.19 inches] at Dundee. To the south of its centre the wind wrought terrible destruction. There were a number of deaths and many places lost all communications with the outside world.

Southport, Lancashire, on the Irish Sea coast was not a place to be at 7AM. The wind was averaging 67 mph, storm force 11 on the Beaufort Scale, and the strongest gust was 92 mph. That exerted a force of around 130-kg on anyone out walking. In Ireland the wind was even stronger and it was thought to be the worst storm since January 1839. At Phoenix Park Dublin nearly 3,000 trees were blown down and in the city itself many houses were unroofed with chimneys demolished. A woman died from falling bricks.

Buildings collapsed including a tenement house in Cork killing a girl and two tall chimneys fell in Belfast seriously injuring two men. Across the Irish Sea at Barrow a train was blown off the Leven Viaduct pushing over 10 carriages and several passengers were hurt. Two lives were lost at Burnley in Lancashire, one being that of a boy hit by a hoarding. Liverpool was virtually cut off from telegraphic communication and many shops had their windows blown in and their wares scattered along the streets.

The wind was so fierce in Holyhead it lifted St Elbon's Church completely off its foundations and it collapsed in ruins.

The storm swept to the north-east coast of England causing death and destruction. The wind blew a sailor into the sea at West Hartlepool and he was drowned; a similar fate befell a worker at Middlesbrough. A wall collapsed in Stockton killing an elderly lady. A further death took place in Newcastle when a chimney toppled through a roof killing a Methodist minister.

February 1903 as a whole was an exceptionally stormy month with one gale following another in northern Britain but it was very mild at 3C above average with little frost and no snow.

Phoenix Park, Dublin suffered the loss of 3,000 trees during the February 27th storm, 1903.

A fine example of Cumulus Congestus that developed further into a heavy shower.
Seen here looking south-west towards Looe in Cornwall, 7th August 2001 at 16-50hrs.
Picture by Mike Mildren.

Giant Weather Balloon Used to Raise Repairman to Tower Top

When an anemometer was damaged atop a 135-foot tower at White Sands Proving Ground, N. Mex., a weather balloon was used in replacing it. The idea to use the balloon in the extraordinary role was conceived when a plan to employ a portable scaffolding to reach the tower's top was discarded as too costly and time-consuming. Operation Balloon worked perfectly and saved an estimated 900 man-hours.

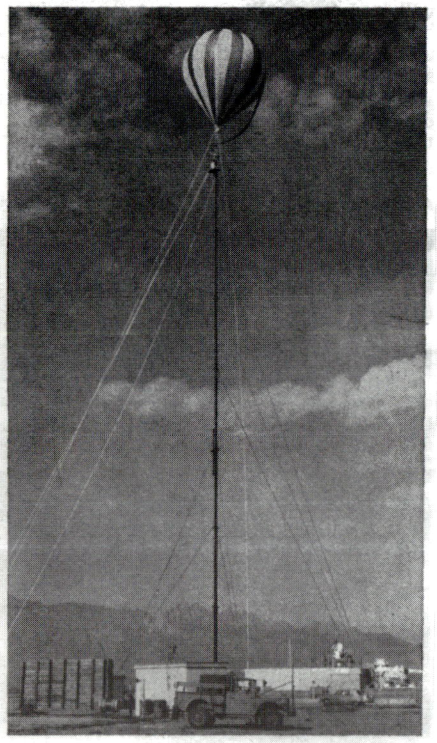

84

POPULAR MECHANICS

JUNE 1958

Yet another interesting newspaper clipping kindly sent in by reader and meterologist Norman Brooks.

An extraordinar

After reading Dave Mutton's excellent Statistical review of the last Millennium I thought it would be appropriate to expand and add a few memories and records to one of the most outstanding weather events of the last century.

In my lifetime there have been a number of memorable weather events. These include the cold and blizzards of 1947, the incredible summer of 1976; the astonishing cold and snow of December 1981; the great storm of 1987, but the one for me which surpassed all others was the great Winter of 1962/3. The prolonged cold created a meteorological phenomenon, unlikely to be equalled for a very long time, if ever.

December 1962 opened with high pressure to the east of the UK and this had started to move SE towards Germany where daytime maximum temperatures were well below freezing. This resulted in a very gentle south-east airstream, which gave England and Wales several days of quiet, cold and foggy weather. This period of cold continental air could have been the precursor of what was to come, but the early cold snap relinquished its grip by the end of the first week. The weather then for the next two weeks was much as we would expect for Mid-December, one short lived burst of maritime arctic air interspersed with seasonal and mild Atlantic winds. On 22nd December ominous pressure changes were occurring, a strong anticyclone over Scandinavia was intensifying and starting to feed in a very cold air steam from the near continent. On the 23rd December 06.OOhrs temperatures in Holland and North Germany were ranging between –13°C & -19°C and a cold front extending from the northern North Sea to SW England was introducing this icy blast into the UK. With the intensifying Scandinavian High and low pressure in the Mediterranean a 'European block' was established. The biting easterly wind gave most of England and Wales a sub-zero maximum on the 23rd December and this was the start of the longest unbroken cold spell ever recorded. Taking the months December / January / February as winter (meteorologically speaking) this ranks as the coldest winter of the last century. January 1963 was certainly the coldest in this period averaging -2.1°C [28.2F] Gordon Manley's Central England statistics refers] though February 1947 with a mean of –1.9°C[28.6F] ranks as the coldest February.

Christmas day dawned very cold over England and Wales with temperatures falling generally to between -5°C [23F] and -10°C [14F] but - 12.2°C [lOF] was recorded at Warsop in Nottinghamshire. Maximum temperatures stayed well below freezing all day including the normally mild South West. A developing trough over Scotland at this time, started to progress south and this introduced the first snow of

Cycling across the Thames, Windsor. January 1963

It is not every day that one has the chance to ride a bicycle on the Thames, but for this cyclist that chance came yesterday at Windsor, where the river is frozen from bank to bank for a considerable distance.

People gazing in wonder at the frozen sea. Herne Bay, January, 1963.

Winter 1962-63

By Cliff Manning.

the spell to most of England and Wales on the 26th December. It was exceptionally deep in the South with a cover of lying snow 30cm-45 cm[12-18 inches] in depth(see weather chart for 0600h 26th December). For many it would be the last week in February before the severe weather started to loosen its grip and the 5th March 1963 when the last traces of snow disappeared from my home town of Bedworth near Nuneaton, Warwickshire, a truly remarkable situation.

Boxing Day was followed by many more memorable falls notably on 29th December when a depression in Biscay tracked northeast and gave much of the Southern half of Britain a blizzard with 6 metre [20-foot drifts] in places. Other substantial falls followed on 3/4 January, 19/20 January and 6/7 February. Snow also fell in between these dates to a lesser degree, but added significantly to the existing cover One of the most vivid recollections I have was the persistence of lying snow despite many gloriously sunny days. There never seemed to be the slightest hint of a thaw with frost more or less every night and many days in my area maintaining maximums below freezing. This posed an enormous problem for road and rail transport. I can remember gritting lorries fighting a losing battle; the normally successful method of keeping main roads clear was totally ineffective and deep ruts of frozen snow and ice were a constant reminder to all travellers that this was no ordinary winter. It was also extremely difficult for pedestrians, footpaths were covered in snow and ice for around nine weeks and the frequent falls of snow made it impossible to keep them clear. The larger towns and cities, normally free from the worst of Arctic weather did not escape and all transport and plant life seemed to carry a perpetual bonnet of snow. Central heating was not the norm at this time and was a luxury enjoyed by relatively few homes. Due to the severity of the cold, many houses had their bedroom windows permanently glazed in frost. I would imagine it would be difficult for our younger generation to accept that this could actually occur in this country, because it certainly resembled a winter scene comparable to Northern Europe rather than the UK.

Snow drifts reached 12 feet high at Sidcot near Winscombe in Somerset. Caroline Sunderland remembers fetching milk by sledge as the milkman could not get up the hill.

Several times during this incredible winter the influence of low pressure near Biscay gave indications of milder air spreading in from southern Europe but each time, easterly winds tightened their grip and any chance of a possible thaw dissipated with more snow and plunging temperatures.

This unique spell of prolonged cold also gave many places in Western Europe their coldest winter of the century. For me it gave an enthusiastic burst of interest and the observations and events will be with me forever.

Note from the Editor: I too was hooked for life and by coincidence received a weather station for a Christmas present. My first reading was an air temperature of minus 4C[25F] during the morning of Boxing Day 1962.

Weather Eye Competition

Generously sponsored by Barometer World, Merton, Devon.

The world's highest recorded barometer reading was measured on the 31st December 1968 at Agata. It was an extraordinary 1083.8mb [hPa] or 32 inches. ***In what country is Agata situated?***

Send in the correct answer to Frosted Earth with your name, address and telephone number clearly labelled and you will be put into our draw that will take place on March 1st 2002. Top Prize a barometer. For other prizes see the Editor's Note page 2.

NAME:

ADDRESS:

TELEPHONE NUMBER: eMail:

ANSWER:

ISSUE 8
Weather
eYe
The frightening facts about LANDSLIDES
Paris reveals its Weather secrets.

Weather eye

"For everybody fascinated by the Weather."

Editor Ian Currie

Subscriptions & back issues to Weather Eye Subscriptions:
77 Rickman Hill, Coulsdon, Surrey CR5 3DT
Tel: 01737 554869 Fax: 01737 554869
Email: iancurrie@frostedearth.com

Front Cover: This scene looks like the aftermath of a severe earthquake. The road west from Coldharbour c the southern slope of Leith Hill, Surrey, has be made impassable by landslips during the reco breaking rains of 2000/1.

Back Cover: Brighton Beach during the afternoon of the 4t September 1999. The temperature had reache 26C-27C over southern England. The month proved the warmest September for 50 years a the sixth warmest back to the 1650s.

Published by: Frosted Earth, 77 Rickman Hill, Coulsdon, Surrey CR5 3DT

Printed by: Litho Techniques Ltd, 46-50 Godstone Road, Whyteleafe, Surrey CR3 0EA

This excellent picture of a cumulonimbus cloud was taken by Mr Edward Quelch at Lingfield, Surrey around 15.30PM GMT on February 28th 2000. It had produced lightning and thunder with a fall of rain and hail. The picture shows a good example of a down draught in the rear of the storm consisting of a curtain of ice crystals and snow flakes which are slowly evaporating. This cools their surfaces down allowing them to penetrate to quite low levels before dissipating. A low pressure system lay to the north of Britain with a showery westerly polar maritime airstream over southern England.

LANDSLIDE BRITAIN

Ian Currie

ISSUE number 7 of Weather eye was devoted to the Autumn 2000 and early Winter Floods. Whilst there was no repeat of the overwhelming rains that so inundated Uckfield, Lewes and York during October and November, rainfall has continued well above average. This has been especially so for southern England with a very wet winter followed by a wet March and April.

Reader Jack Pope's summary of winter rain at his Crawley Down Weather Station in West Sussex illustrates the point. The following is his synopsis.

"I am writing this summary on the first day of statistical spring [March 1st]. The winter [Dec.-Feb] was very wet [180% of the long-term average-LTA] with some 414mm of rain falling on 50 days. All this deluged onto saturated ground after the unbelievably wet autumn 2000 when 610mm of rain fell, 234% of the LTA. Together autumn and winter rain totalled 1024mm against a LTA of 491mm. The average for the whole year is 864mm".

As a result of all this rain Britain is crumbling. An unprecedented number of landslides have torn huge chunks from cliffs, cuttings, embankments and even hills. Over 500 according to the British Geological Survey- a figure that is sure to rise.

The rain has built up tremendous pressure within the pores of the spongy chalk and sandstone. Where there is a layer of clay underneath the water can cause the overlying rocks to slip off. In less porous rocks there are still cracks and fissures and water has entered and filled them. Occasional frosts have generated terrific pressures when the water froze. This loosened the rock face sending thousands of

The London-Brighton railway line passes through the North Downs in a steep sided cutting before entering a tunnel. It suffered frequent landslips and the line was closed on several occasions as in this picture on Sunday 11th February 2001. Work at restoring traffic is nearing completion. After the record breaking wet autum and heavy rains of December and January 73mm of rain fell in the first 10 days of February.

tonnes of rock hurtling downhill. In other places it is a slow creep, an ooze inching slowly forward but still a mighty force involving vast amounts of soil and rock.

Nefyn on the Lleyn peninsula, North Wales, was the scene of a tragic landslide on the 2nd January 2001 when a person died and another was badly injured. A couple who had moved to the area for their retirement were sitting in a vehicle parked at a cliff top car park overlooking the beach. Suddenly the cliff behind them gave way forcing their car against railings. They were trapped inside the car and then a further slip sent them and an unoccupied vehicle plunging 60-metres to the beach below. Another couple at the car park saw the approaching mud and fled from their van which sustained some damage.

The cliffs here comprise of alternating layers of sand, gravel and clay and tend to become very unstable in persistent wet weather. Before the slide at Nefyn there was a spell of freeze-thaw conditions.

All round the coast there have been huge cliff falls though fortunately not as tragic as Nefyn but larger in terms of material on the move. A week before the North Wales incident a million tonnes of cliff collapsed at Charmouth in Dorset. At the end of January it was the turn of the White Cliffs of Dover when a section the size of a super tanker

Cracks and fissures run across country on the south side of Leith Hill, Surrey. Underlying clays lubricated by month's of heavy rain provided a slip off slope for the sandstone above.

collapsed. In March Shanklin on the Isle of Wight suffered a dreadful slide which injured several guests at the Shanklin Beach Hotel. Tonnes of debris thrust onto the dance floor at a packed Saturday evening function.

A famous coastal landmark has disappeared. At the beginning of April The Devil's Chimney, Beachy Head, Sussex, a well-known 60-metre high edifice, tottered and then tumbled into the foaming English Channel.

Landslips have not been confined to coasts. Leith Hill at just under 300 metres, Southeast England's highest point, is on the move. Its southern flank south-west of the village of Coldharbour is slipping. This is not new, as a glance at the Ordnance Survey map of the area will show. The word `landslip' is actually marked on it. It is a classic rotational slip point where in this case hard chert beds overlie softer sands and clays. Here masses of rock slip vertically downwards whilst the front or toe rides upwards lubricated by water. From mid September to April the hill has had over 1100mm[43 inches] of rain. This triggered the worst landslip for centuries.

The road leading from the village runs through an area that resembles scenes from an earthquake zone. In places the road has either been heaved upwards or thrust downwards. Fissures criss –cross the road surface and run for several hundred metres. Large trees have toppled or are about to keel over. The road around the hill may never be a through route again.

There have been 40 landslides since September on the National rail network. The deep cuttings on the approach to the tunnels under the North Downs in Surrey and Kent have suffered badly. On the roads there have been 60 major slips. One is on the M25 near junction 6 where springs have burst out and caused the scarp slope to slump. In many cases Man has been powerless to stop the forces of Nature.

With the rains continuing through April slides and rock falls could persist well into the summer and come back with a vengeance if there is another wet autumn.

Scene of the tragic landslide at Nefyn early January 2001. Picture by Arwyn Roberts of the Caernarfon and Denbigh Herald.

FLAVOURS OF BRAZIL

Pictures taken by Mr Peter Cann. See text.

Mr. Peter Cann visited a Weather display set up by the editor at Selsdon Country Day in August 1999 and bought a thermometer from him. The instrument was to go on a long journey. Mr. Cann takes up the story:

My visit to Brazil in April 2000 was to carry out an initial survey of the dragonflies in the area as part of the Cameroon Dragonfly Project. The group mainly carries out field studies in Africa; this year was the first visit to Brazil. The study was a great success, finding a wide range of species and established a survey that will hopefully continue into the future. The group's visits and findings can be found on their *Web Site www.macromia.com*

Our location, Guapi Acu, lay 50 miles north east of Rio de Janeiro within Brazil's Atlantic rain forest. This is one of the most threatened habitats in the world, just 2% remains. These lowlands resemble the rolling hills of Sussex. At 500

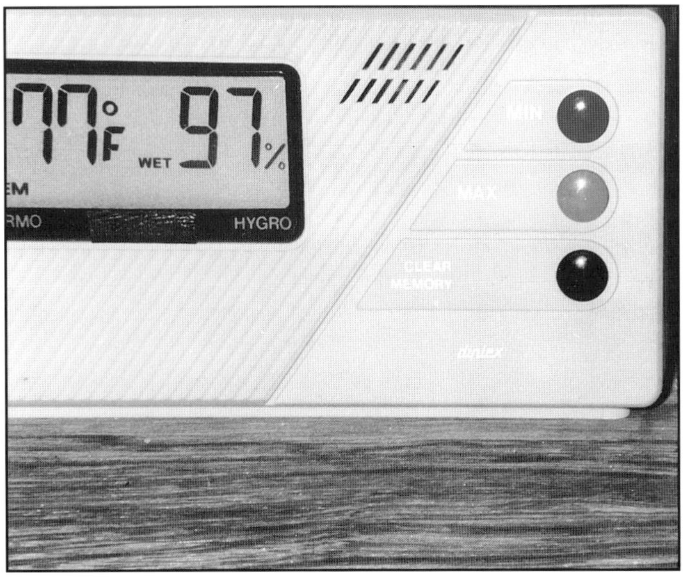

feet you are on the edge of the rain forest, which clothes the mountains.

Our camp was at the edge of this forest, the nearest summit some 7600 feet high, is about 5 miles north. There are many fast flowing streams from the mountains, this being our water supply. When drinking it we added an iodine tablet in case of any bugs. When walking under the rain forest's canopy the humidity rises dramatically, you perspire profusely, so drinking regularly is essential. The temperature and hygro chart shows the enervating atmosphere. My measurements were taken under an open sided veranda using an electronic Hygrometer and max/min thermometer purchased from Mr. Currie. Sitting out on the veranda was a sheer delight, the chirping of the crickets and at night the flashing of the fireflies made it a very rewarding experience, not to mention the rich variety of birds and other creatures.

Our treks into the rain forest were quite strenuous, on some days the mountains would be cloaked in mist and cloud, distant thunder would be followed by torrential rain. The sky quickly cleared and the humidity became stifling.

In all, the trip was very successful for the entomological studies as well as experiencing first hand the Brazilian rain forest.

My memories are best summarized by a quotation from Albert Einstein, "the most beautiful thing we can experience is the mysterious. It is the source of all true art and science".

Mr Peter Cann's Temperature and Humidity Readings from Guapi Acu-Brazil. April 3rd to April 15th 2000.

Date	Max Temps °C	Min Temps °C	Midday Temps °C	Hygro % Midday
Mon 3rd	26	20	26	81
Tue 4th	28	20	23	93
Weds 5th	27	21	27	85
Thurs 6th	29	23	29	70
Fri 7th	29	21	29	85
Sat 8th	32	22	31	69
Sun 9th	32	23	32	62
Mon 10th	32	27	30	65
Tue 11th	29	22	28	76
Wed 12th	34	25	34	61
Thurs 13th	31	24	29	86
Fri 14th	29	24	29	84
Sat 15th			29	74

WHEN THE OILSKIN FROZE

Weather eye is very grateful to Mrs Geddie of Meopham, Kent, for providing details of an extraordinary incident involving an antique cabinet that took place at Kingsdown near Dover during a severe gale in January 1978. Weather eye went to the village to find out more.

Between Kingsdown and Ramsgate, lying 4 miles offshore, is a series of sandbanks that have a reputation unrivalled anywhere in the world. Since the Middle Ages literally thousands of ships have been lost on what was known to medieval mariners as the `dreaded shippe swallower', the Goodwin Sands. Even today Trinity House marks their position some nine miles in length, with three light ships and 15 buoys.

In the days of sail and with the absence of modern navigational aides there were several lifeboat stations in the area. The one at Kingsdown existed from 1866 to 1927 and was responsible for many hundreds of lives being saved. In February 1870 a fierce and freezing southeast gale wrecked the fully rigged 1600-ton ship the Glendura. Jarvist Arnold the remarkable and legendary coxswain in the lifeboat Sabrina made four trips out to the ship. Each journey a fresh crew was used but Jarvist remained at the helm and everyone on board the stricken vessel was saved. When at last he took off his oilskins they were frozen so stiff they stood quite upright in the lifeboat house.
He made another astonishing rescue on the night of the 17th December 1872.

A night so stormy that slates and chimney pots were pulled from the roofs of tiny cottages that clustered around the foreshore at Kingsdown. The steamship Sorrento foundered and mountainous seas broke over the ship. Pieces of the ship were being torn away with every wave. Perched on the tiny bridge were 31 crew plus half of the Walmer lifeboat's compliment. It had joined in the rescue but had been parted from the Sorrento when a tough five-inch cable snapped. The tiny Kingsdown lifeboat managed to draw alongside in horrendous circumstances and with Coxswain Jarvist Arnold skillfully holding her steady they took everyone off. Minutes later the steamer could bear the pounding no longer, and with a terrific grinding groan split in two and disappeared forever. The courage and seamanship displayed remains one of the great events in the history of the Lifeboat Service.

Kingsdown lifeboat station closed on the 7th January 1927 and her fourth lifeboat the Charles Hargreaves was moved to Walmer. The station was then converted into a private dwelling as it is today but there remains a close association with the sea. None more so than on the 11th and 12th January 1978. A vicious area of low pressure moved quickly across England. [See page 18-19 of issue 7]. Gusts of wind reached hurricane force and huge seas destroyed Margate Pier. Tonnes of shingle were swept into the lounge of the old lifeboat station. At the same time an antique Austrian cabinet, inset with many small drawers was washed from the room right out onto the Goodwin Sands.

Amazingly the cabinet was recovered and only ONE drawer was missing. The original pre war carpet was laid out on the beach to dry and was able to be used again. The French doors and windows had to be replaced, as did the balcony that faced out to sea. Further storms lashed the house and the balcony has now been partly taken down.

The old Lifeboat House has been immortalized in the film Isadora Duncan starring Vanessa Redgrave. It was shot in the house and surrounding beach. But the real dramas were those fought at sea by the valiant crews from the lifeboat station on the beach: and that oilskin standing upright after Jarvist Arnold returned from the freezing Goodwins.

The former life boat station at Kingsdown, Kent, now a private dwelling.

PINNACLES IN THE DESERT

This excellent sunset picture was taken in the south west of Sri Lanka by Mrs Carole Barlow of Alton-Hants.

REPORTS FROM DOWN UNDER

Sheila Marks of Coulsdon, Surrey, took this unusual picture in the Pinnacles Desert, Nambung National Park-Western Australia, about 160 miles north of Perth. It shows cumulus cloud with lenticular or wave cloud above. This indicates a more humid layer of air with a shear in the wind flow, that is a change of speed and direction with height. The temperature at the time was as high as 47C[116F].

The strange pinnacle shaped limestone rocks in the picture have an interesting origin. The raw material for them came in the form of seashells from an earlier epoch rich in marine life. The shells have been broken down by the elements into lime-rich sand and winds have blown the sand into dunes that have advanced inland.

Rain washing through the sands formed a layer of soft limestone with the coarser and harder quartz sandstone above. Vegetation then stabilised the dunes building up a layer of soil and humus which in turn through leaching produced a hard band of calcrete.

Cracks developed in this calcrete layer and were enlarged by plant roots enabling the penetration of winter rains into the soft limestone below, leaching some of it away. Subsequent removal of the sand by prevailing winds has exposed the remaining soft limestone, still protected by its cap of calcrete.

In this area most of the annual rainfall of 600mm falls from May to September.

A REVIEW OF THE CENTURY'S WEAT

Summary and Data compiled by David M

Although most people celebrated the passing of the Millennium on 31st December 1999, it is only on 1st January 2001 that the new Millennium begins. In fact the year 2000 is the last of the twentieth century and not the first of the twenty-first. Now is therefore an appropriate time to look back over some of the highlights, and the low-lights, of Leicestershire's weather from 1901-2000. Few places are able to do this but Leicestershire has one of the country's longest periods of continuous weather records, from 1836 for temperature and rainfall and from 1896 for sunshine.

At Wistow, weather records began in 1836 and at the Towers Hospital in Leicester in 1871. At Leicester Museum records were kept from 1875 to 1899. At the turn of the century weather records were still being kept at the Towers Hospital and at Belvoir Castle from 1900 to 1934. Daily weather observations at the Towers Hospital continued from 1870 to 1960 and only ceased when the head gardener retired. Between 1910 and 1960 there were a number of rainfall only stations mostly run by water authorities at sewage farms and reservoirs.

The weather over the past 100 years has also undergone significant changes and generated much interest.

In 1901 the whole "Global Warming" issue lay decades ahead but as the century closed it had become our great preoccupation.

The end of the century was warmer than its beginning by just over one degree Celsius. Warming occurred in two stages, between 1980 and 2000 and again between 1930 and 1950. Temperatures were steady in the first few years of the century and again between 1950 and 1980 at which many scientists were worried not about global warming but about global cooling and a descent into the next Ice Age! On the other hand annual rainfall totals show no trend, just a good deal of year-by-year variation. We can detect no evidence of wetter or drier conditions to accompany the warming. Throughout the century the annual mean temperature has been 9.5 C or 49.2 F, while the annual mean rainfall has been 688.1 millimetres or 26.65 inches. Total annual sunshine over the 100 years came out at 1314.7 hours.

Of more interest are the extreme conditions. Some of these events fall within the memory of today's residents, but some are long gone. Many will recall the century's wettest day, July 10th 1968 when 70.4 mm or 2.77 inches of rain fell. There was also 50.8 mm or 2.00 inches recorded on 15th July 1937.

Some memories might go back to the cold winters of the 1940s. January 1940 was the 3rd coldest month of the

The Cosby Brook photographed by David Mutton on 14th January 1982 after Leicestershire had recorded its coldest night of the 20th century when the air temperature dropped to –19.5C.

WEATHER MEANS, HIGHS AND LOWS FOR COSBY WEATHER STATION: 1901 - 2000

Temperature °C

MEAN Temps °C	9.5	DATE
Warmest year	10.6	1990
Coldest year	8.1	1917
Warmest Month	19.7	1997 Aug.
Coldest Month	-2.7	1947 Feb.
Warmest Day	35.5	9th August 1911
Coldest Night	-19.5	14th January 1982

Weather eye is grateful to David Mutton for h

R : 1901 to 2000 IN LEICESTERSHIRE

on. FRMetS. COSBY WEATHER STATION

century and came in the middle of a very cold and snowy month that saw temperatures regularly plunge to over ten degrees below freezing. The following winter was little better and witnessed one of the heaviest snowfalls on record. Snow began on 17th February 1941 and the storm continued until 20th by which time the snow lay to a depth of 2 feet in the city and up to 4 feet deep in the country. For sheer persistence of snow cover the winter of 1947 has few rivals. Leicester had a level cover of 4 feet with 10-foot drifts in many places. Snow cover was complete by 21st January and remained until mid-March when the thaw eventually set in. February 1947 with a daily mean temperature of -2.7 C (27.2 F) was the coldest month of the century. The melting snow caused severe flooding during the spring but the following summer was hot and dry.

On the brighter side, the heat waves of August 1911 and August 1990 will long be recalled. A close look at the records reveals some real oddities. The summer of 1959 was hot and sunny and this weather continued well into October. There were several drought summers in the 1970s. 1975 and 1976 produced long periods of dry and hot weather with water shortages in a number of areas.

On the other hand Leicester suffered some severe flooding especially in the Saffron Lane area, after 70.4 mm [2.77 inches] of rain was recorded on 10th July 1968. In the 100 years since 1901, this was the wettest day of any in Leicestershire.

Records of sunshine began in Leicestershire in 1896. Some interesting figures emerged as I browsed through the figures. The sunniest month of the century was July 1911 with 273 hours beating June 1957 by 3 hours. 'The dullest month was December 1902 when only 6 hours was recorded. The sunniest year was 1959 with 1715 hours closely followed by 1989 with 1697 hours. Annual mean sunshine total over the l00 years was 1314.7 hours, and the total average for the new 30-year period (1971 to 2000) is 1369.4 hours.

If we take the first 10 years of the century, 1901 to 1910, the total sunshine hours came out at 12971 hours. The last 10 years of the century 1991 to 2000 produced 14408 hours of sunshine. This higher total by some 1437 hours is probably due to Clean Air Acts being brought in and less industrial pollution than there was at the turn of the century.

We might ask what the future holds? Scientists tell us to expect warmer conditions, more storms and floods in the autumns with drier summers. But our weather is an uncertain creature and the last century has shown what surprises it can hold. Only time will tell if the scientists are right.

infall in mm

an Rainfall mm	688.1	DATE
ettest Year	927.0	2000
iest Year	490.1	1921
ettest Month	190.7	July 1915
iest Month	1.0	Feb. 1959
ettest Day	70.4	10th July 1968

Sunshine in hours.

Mean Sunshine hrs.	1314.7	DATE
Sunniest Year	1715.0	1959
Dullest Year	963.0	1902
Sunniest Month	273.0	July 1911
Dullest Month	6.0	Dec. 1902

summary and welcomes other contributions from readers who have facts and figures for their local area.

Paris reveals its Weather secrets.

Statue of the soldier known as the 'Zouave' at the Pont de l'Alma bridge across the river Seine. In the great 1910 flood the water came up to the tip of his beard.

Last October brought me to Paris for a Weekend to celebrate my 25th Wedding Anniversary. Not a time perhaps to concentrate on weather matters but to enjoy the ambiance of one of the world's most exciting and romantic capitals.

However a stroll through the streets soon revealed that floods, freezes and tempests have beset the city and even provided inspiration to artists of world repute. Whilst experiments on the Weather have been carried out in the very heart of Paris.

Our first morning involved a short walk to the gardens of the Palais de Luxembourg. Formerly the haunt of a ghostly thirteenth century highwayman, a monastery was then built on the site. A palace for Queen Marie de Medici followed in the seventeenth century whilst at the latter end of the eighteenth century it became a prison during the French Revolution. Now it is the seat of the Senate, where the 319 members of the French Upper House meet.

The gardens were battered by the great storm of the 26th December 1999. Damaging gusts of wind reached 104 mph in Paris as an intense low-pressure system crossed northern France causing immense disruption and injury. All commuter train services were shut down, as were half the Paris Metro lines. Across France 33 people were killed and along with a further storm taking a more southerly track destroyed 100 million trees. As in the October 1987 great gale across southern England many trees were left in a weakened state and notices were put up around the gardens to warn the public of

A warning of unsafe trees in the gardens of the Palais de Luxembourg.

the possible risk of injury by falling branches in windy conditions.

We then walked to the Isle de Cité area, an island within the river Seine famous for the Cathedral of Notre Dame, but it was the nearby Saint Chapelle that was of special interest. One can only gaze in awe on seeing the remarkable glow of its wondrous 13th century windows that intensify the merest hint of a sunbeam. On the walls of nearby streets were plaques to mark the Great Flood of January 1910, a bench mark flood reaching 9 metres above the mean watermark. Later that day we put our 3-day Metro tickets to good use by going to a Post Card Fair at the Porte de Champerret. Dealers had boxes and boxes of cards devoted to these floods illustrating the significance of the event.

Flood at Port Marley[1887] by Alfred Sisley

A flood marker within the Isle de Cité.

H Warner in his book "Scenes from the Paris Flood of 1910" described the start of the inundation *"At ten minutes to eleven on the morning of Friday, January 21, 1910 the power station from which all the public clocks of Paris are worked from compressed air was flooded by the Seine. All the clocks stopped simultaneously with military exactitude. With a start of surprise Parisians began to realise that the Seine in flood was not a harmless spectacle that could be watched with the cheerful calm of philosophic detachment, and that the river in revolt was an enemy to be feared even by the most civilised city in Europe".*

Most of the river basin of the river Seine is formed of permeable rocks, the absorptive capacity of which mitigates the risk of river floods. The Seine is the most regular of the major rivers of France and the most naturally

'Melting of the ice on the Seine' painted from a sketch by Monet during January 1880. Before the thaw came he chopped holes in the ice to set up his easel. Both December 1879 and January 1880 were months of severe cold.

navigable. Occasionally the summer level is considerably reduced (such as in the summers of 1947 and 1949), but the sandbanks that are so typical of the Loire do not appear. Low water is further masked by the regularization of the river that has been carried out to improve its navigability. Winter floods are rarely dangerous, but in January 1910 exceptionally heavy rainfall caused the river to rise to levels not seen since February 1658 flooding the extensive low-lying quarters along its ancient meander loop (the Marais). In January 1924 and also in January 1955 the river again rose to more than 7 metres in Paris. The average flow at Paris is about 2800 cubic metres per second, as compared with the 1910 flood rate of about 83,000 and the 1947 and 1949 minimums of about 700.

A short walk across the Seine and you can see the Tour St. Jacques, a flamboyant Gothic bell tower built for the powerful 16th- century Butcher's guild. In 1648, Blaise Pascal[1623-62] used the tower to repeat his barometric experiments that he originally carried out on the Puy-de-Dome. Due to ill health Pascal persuaded his younger brother to carry a Torricelli tube to the top of the 1400 metres high mountain. The level fell 84mm and thus showed the existence of atmospheric pressure and that it falls near the surface by approximately 25mm [1 inch] per 300metres[1000 feet]. Pascal's chief work was concerned with fluid pressure. He stated that pressure everywhere within a fluid is the same, and pressure applied at one point is transmitted equally. We all make use of this when we drive a car and put our foot on the brake. His name is immortalized on modern barometers by the unit of pressure the pascal[Pa].

The Tour St. Jacques stands in a small park that is now fittingly a Weather Station.

A short walk from our hotel brought us to the Musee d'Orsay. Formerly an elegant railway terminus it inspired other stations to be modelled after it. One artist called it somewhat prophetically a "palace of fine arts". Now it has been transformed into a remarkable museum with its impressionist paintings the greatest attraction. My wife had to virtually drag me out of the building. The reason is that among the exhibits were a number of works of art depicting the weather at a time when the elements were in extreme mode. Monet was inspired by severe winter weather in 1879 and January 1880. He would paint out in the open coming in frozen stiff, his coat and trousers like boards and hair a mass of icicles. Not surprising as the temperature had been as low as minus 28C at Orleans just south of Paris during 1879. Another contemporary artist greatly influenced by Monet was Alfred Sisley and he produced some excellent Weather canvases such as

Top left and bottom: Post cards capturing dramatic scenes from the 1910 flood.

The Tour St. Jacques used by Blaise Pascal to repeat the barometric experiments originally carried out on the Puy-de-Dome. In the foreground is a modern weather station.
Opposite Another postcard from Paris illustrating the 1910 flood.

Flood at Port-Marley[1887].

In the 1910 floods the Seine actually flowed through the Orsay terminus as the water poured onto the line higher up the river. It then fell back into the Seine through the ventilation shafts of the station, which looked for all the world like a swimming bath. Only the iron gallery, on a level with the entrance from the road, was left unsubmerged; the central depth had been converted into a huge tank of muddy water, while the sightseer looked vainly for the engines and carriages that lay drowned beneath.

After a short stroll west along the Quai d'Orsay one comes to the Pont de l'Alma. The bridge has a sculpture of a Second Empire Soldier, known as the Zouave. For decades the figure has been used to gauge the water level of the Seine. In the great inundation of 1910, he was submerged to the tip of his beard.

The weather conditions during our Weekend in Paris had been somewhat tame compared to the situation in England. This was the occasion of the Bognor tornado followed by a major low heading towards England later on Sunday. We were glad we travelled under the Channel for there was a gale blowing by evening and our Eurostar Train was one of the last to get through to Waterloo. Later that night trains were held up by floodwater in Kent. We had to battle our way home from the local station in lashing rain and strong winds. Paris seemed so far away.

The end of a fine weather day in Paris- with stratocumulus perlucidus at sunset 26th October 2000 from the Pont d' l'Alma

An anemometer used on a pub sign at Chatham Green, just north of Chelmsford, Essex.

This old advert. for PYE Radio, was kindly sent in by Mr. Norman Brooks, of Dover. It was placed in *The Listener* of the 22nd April 1943.

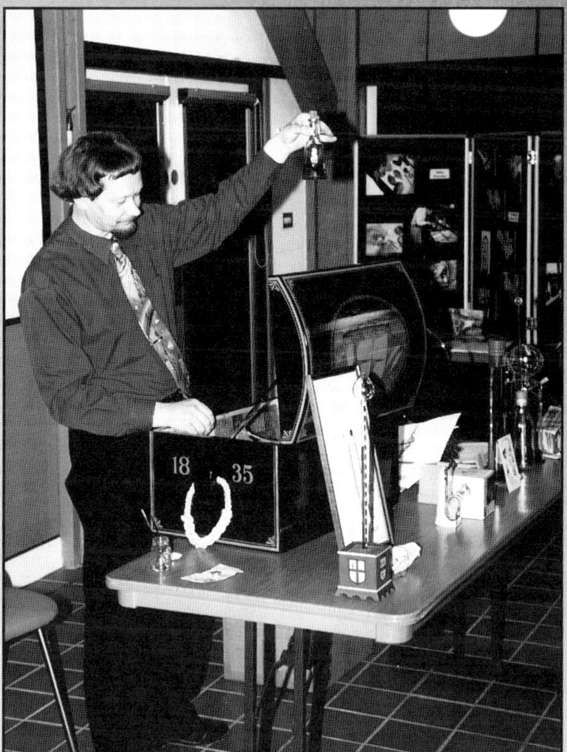

Mr Philip Collins of Barometer World, giving an intriguing talk on old weather instruments at Rosemoor Gardens, Devon in September 2000. Editor Ian Currie also gave a talk as part of a "*Weather Day*". It is hoped to be repeated in 2002. Contact Weather eye for details.

FOR HIRE
PIMM'S

Weather eye

ISSUE 7

FLOOD SPECIAL

UCKFIELDS DAY OF DRAMA

YORK'S HIGHEST FLOOD

LEWES UNDER SEIGE

1000 YEARS OF FLOODS AND TEMPESTS

£2.50

Weather eye

"For everybody fascinated by the Weather."

Editor Ian Currie

Subscriptions & back issues to Weather Eye Subscriptions:
77 Rickman Hill, Coulsdon, Surrey CR5 3DT
Tel: 01737 554869 Fax: 01737 554869
Email: ian.currie@frostedearth.com

Front Cover: A shed carried several miles by the raging torrent collides with a Rover 216 in view of a fire fighting rescue team near Uckfield Station o the 12th October 2000. Picture by John Elms.

Back Cover: The Millennium Floods did provide some reflective moments as here near Pulborough, West Sussex, on the 3rd of November 2000. The River Arun's flood plain had become a vast lake. Picture by Ian Currie

Published by: Frosted Earth, 77 Rickman Hill, Coulsdon, Surrey CR5 3DT

Printed by: Litho Techniques Ltd, 46-50 Godstone Road, Whyteleafe, Surrey CR3 0EA

St Nicholas Church reflecting onto deceptively tranquil waters after the River Wey burst its banks in Guildford, Surrey, November 7th 2000. 50mm of rain fell in 24 hours. on the Wey catchment.

THE MILLENNIUM FLOODS AUTUMN 2000

Ian Currie

AT THE end of August, my garden water butt was almost empty. Contrary to popular belief, many parts of the British Isles had enjoyed a drier than average summer. At my Coulsdon based weather station in Surrey the period, June–August, measured just 83 per cent of the long-term average rainfall. By the 13th September this had dropped to 75 percent. Summer was still with us, the mercury had soared to almost 27C on the 11th and reached 29C [84F] at Hawarden Bridge in Flintshire.

What happened next was extraordinary. By the 8th November my weather station had measured its wettest ever autumn at 416 mm with local records extending back 150 years. In Sussex, it was even wetter with totals over 550mm. With an unparalleled 50 severe flood warnings issued by the Environment Agency on one day alone the so-called Millennium Floods had gripped the nation.

The first outstanding event occurred on the 15th September when a low pressure system moved north east across southern England. Rain became torrential over central southern and southeast England. In just a few hours 60mm of rain fell in the Portsmouth area and there was severe flooding in Southsea. The intensity of the rain caused the breakdown of a sewerage pumping station which led to over a metre of polluted water flooding parts of the town. Walderton in West Sussex recorded 84mm [3.4 inches] of rain by 1800hrs.

At my weather station, the day resembled in a somewhat less dramatic mode a tropical storm. For the morning became increasingly wet with strong winds from the south to south east culminating in a furious deluge that led to widespread flooding. The main A23 road was blocked at Redhill and there were 100 flood-related calls to the Surrey Fire and Rescue Service. By mid afternoon the sky dramatically cleared with bright sunshine and calm conditions. We were literally in the `eye'. Encircling the horizon was a wall of towering storm cloud and it was the advancing western edge that looked particularly menacing. Soon rumbles of thunder were heard, the sunlight faded and a breeze stirred. Lightning followed, darting across a rapidly darkening sky. Several hours of storm ensued with rain, heavy but not torrential. It was hurled at the windows by a gusty north west wind.

I had recorded 53mm of rain by midnight, the wettest September day since 1973.

Mid afternoon on the 15th September 2000 in Church Street, Reigate and the busy A25 was almost impassable. Picture by Mark Davison.

THE REST of September was wet with 25mm [1 inch] of rain being recorded on 10 of the last 15 days somewhere in the British Isles from Southampton to Lerwick and for many it was the wettest September since 1981. By the end of the month my water butt had been filled several times over.

Steady rain falling on thirsty ground does great benefit and soaks in well. Prolonged torrential rain falling on saturated ground can spell disaster.

On the 9th October a low-pressure system moved across Ireland into Cumbria deepening as it went. 57mm of rain fell at Wroxall on the Isle of Wight and 80 properties were flooded at Ryde. Some 49 Flood warnings were issued throughout southern England. Another secondary low developed and moved into Cornwall on the 10th with further rain across the south and as it moved gently north-east into the Midlands it slowly intensified. The stage was set for some remarkable weather.

The 11th had been deceptively sunny during the morning. Heavy showers developed later in the afternoon. Around 18.30 hrs as evening was closing in I was travelling by car along the Hog's Back in Surrey, that wonderful weather vantage-point between Guildford and Farnham. Looking south, I gazed in awe at a magnificent line of cumulo nimbus [thunderclouds] towering in a majestic line of Himalayan proportions. Heavy showers were aligned over Sussex, Kent and Surrey coming in off the warm waters of the Channel. Later that night as I was heading south on the M25 flashes of lightning revealed those angry 'mountains'. They were still there, and very potent producing veritable cascades of rain. After midnight in Coulsdon occasionally a deluge would strike my house but further south over Sussex the rain kept going, downpour after downpour; a months worth of rain, two months rain- on it went and when daylight came a disaster began to unfold.

Parts of Sussex had a phenomenal total of over 200mm [8 inches] of rain in 60 hours and indeed most fell in just 12 hours. Some of the heaviest rain was measured in the source area of several river systems, the Medway, Ouse, Rother and Beult. Flood water surged down the whole course of these rivers and near the coast was prevented from draining away quickly by high tides.

I visited Lewes, East Sussex, during Thursday evening of the 12th and it was a surreal scene. Streetlights reflected onto the rising waters of the river Ouse which had overwhelmed the High Street. I watched as water lapped across the floor of a clothes shop slowly soaking the hems of garments hanging on clothes racks. Further along, a bank was awash with water knee deep at the counters. In the distance, I thought a boat was approaching. As it glided towards me like a ghost ship, I saw it was actually an empty builder's skip. It turned several circles before disappearing into the night.

A super market was completely inundated. Cars still parked outside were submerged almost up to their bonnets and in the short time it took to photograph the scene water rose over the door locks. Higher up the High Street and safe from the deepest flood hundreds of people were spending the night at the Town Hall. Volunteers including the Mayor, served hot drinks and food, registered the evacuees' names and helped the frail brought in by ambulance. It was an extraordinary scene, a cat meowed in its basket, a child played with plastic building bricks, people sat huddled and dazed and a man told of his car disappearing under the murky waters.

At Madehurst in Sussex, the heavy rain had ruined a crop of linseed and there was no recourse but to burn it and then plough the remains in.

The floods in the central Weald were possibly the most extreme for at least a century. In the upper Medway valley the volume of flow approaching Tonbridge, Kent, exceeded the catastrophic floods of 1968 when 225 cubic metres per sec passed through the town. The Leigh Flood Barrier completed in 1981 had to be opened to stem the tide into the rapidly-filling reservoir. At peak capacity it can hold 5,580,000 cubic metres of water. Three of the 5.7 metres high gates were raised for a time allowing 240 cubic metres per second to pass out.

A few weeks before the Floods I had given a talk in Lamberhurst, Kent called 'Droughts, Deluges and Dust-Devils' and left my car outside the village hall. On National Television News, I saw a boat sail by over the same parking bay.

The River Arun took the form of a huge lake as it flowed through the South Downs, as seen here from Bury Hill, West Sussex. Picture by Mark Davison.

UCKFIELD GOES UNDER

by Mark Davison

Cars were swept away outside Uckfield Station after torrential overnight storms on the 12th October 2000. The river Uck burst its banks and surged through the lower part of the town. Picture by John Elms.

THURSDAY October 12th 2000 was an extraordinary day in East Sussex. Through out the night there had been violent thunderstorms and merciless torrents of rain. Many people could not sleep, so great was the noise. The tropical-style storms seemed to go on all night.

The River Uck, which flows through the lower end of the town was already in full spate following some of the wettest autumnal weather on record. On occasions in the past, including November 1974 and December 1993, the Uck had burst its banks sending waves of water washing into the High Street. But the inundation of the millennium year was beyond anything experienced in people's lifetimes.

By daybreak, the town was virtually marooned, but some people managed to get through the floods to reach their workplace. Still, the rain was falling and in the hours that followed, some of the most dramatic events in Uckfield's history were about to unfold.

Suddenly a wall of water surged into the High Street and industrial estate, smashing shop windows and sweeping a man off his feet into the raging waters.

The story was graphically told on BBC's Southern Counties Radio later that day by reporter John Hunt, who arrived at the height of the drama. Here is his sensational account.

"When I got to Uckfield, I could not believe what I was seeing. There was serious flooding in the High Street. It was difficult to understand the full scale of it, and it was only after an hour I realized. The river had spilled right across a large area of Uckfield, including the industrial estate.

"The most remarkable thing is the speed it happened. A chap was working in Somerfield supermarket, at the back. He heard a bit of a bang and the shutters suddenly buckled and a huge torrent of water came pouring through. That was the first he knew and that was the moment the River Uck burst its banks and sent huge, fast-moving torrents of water bursting through the store. Huge freezers were knocked off their stands throwing all the stock against the front windows. Within 10 minutes, he was up to his waist .The staff rushed upstairs to seek shelter .A new river of water started flowing very fast through the town. It was very dangerous. A man was taken off his feet and swept away.

"The supermarket's front windows suddenly gave way with a huge explosion and the stock from inside came out into the High Street and was bobbing about all over the place. The water was up to the pushbutton of the pedestrian crossing, one meter high, and moving very fast and causing eddies and whirlpools as it went round corners. People were stuck upstairs.

"Later the RNLI put ladders up and rescued people but even they were having difficulty against the strong current of water.

"If the lifeboat cannot make it very easily up the current, what chance was there of people making it?

"I was watching people clearing up in a computer shop. All the computers were submerged in water.The cost is going to be enormous.

"Ann Young, of Oliver's Meadow, had only just renovated her house and had new sofas and carpets. She has got to start all over again.

"It was quite unbelievable. It was such a huge expanse of water that filled the town. Near Tesco's, by the industrial estate, people were standing on a wall, watching. The wall was 400 to 500ft long and it was full of people. Everybody in the town was there with video recorders and cameras. It was as if there was a drama unfolding in front of them and they could not bear to miss a moment of it.

"The fire brigade and RNLI broke into the back of Boots. They feared looting and drugs could be washed down the street and picked up by kids. They were worried drugs may get into the water system.

"It was extraordinary I've never seen anything like it. There were kids aged five or six on a wall that was only a few inches from the incredibly fast-flowing river. They were fishing for things that had been washed out of the supermarket – bars of soap; cans of lager. They were collecting them on this wall. There was a moment when one of them nearly fell in. I could not believe how incredibly dangerous it was. They really did not understand the danger. If the lifeboat could not cope, how could a five-year-old if he fell in?"

Mr Hunt said that the front of the bookshop had caved in and emergency services were helping some people to safety. And it was not long before camera crews and satellite dishes arrived as the media turned up to record the event.

The rain fell all morning and only eased off after lunchtime. There had been further rumbles of thunder and flashes of lightning as the storms departed with a sting in their tail. More than six inches (150mms) had been measured in parts of East Sussex in just 24 hours; the equivalent of two months' rainfall.

In its wake, there were some unforgettable scenes. The roundabout outside McDonalds and Halfords had completely vanished and the water was up to the chevron signs. A vast sea of murky water four-feet deep swirled through the 400-unit business park, bearing hundreds of shop-soiled goods and bottled drinks. At one point the RNLI in their inflatable, had to negotiate the roundabout and potentially perilous submerged fences. It was reported that even supermarket fresh chickens were spotted among the flotsam and jetsam. Children were scolded for picking up chocolate bars from the flood and eating them, risking sickness from the contaminated water.

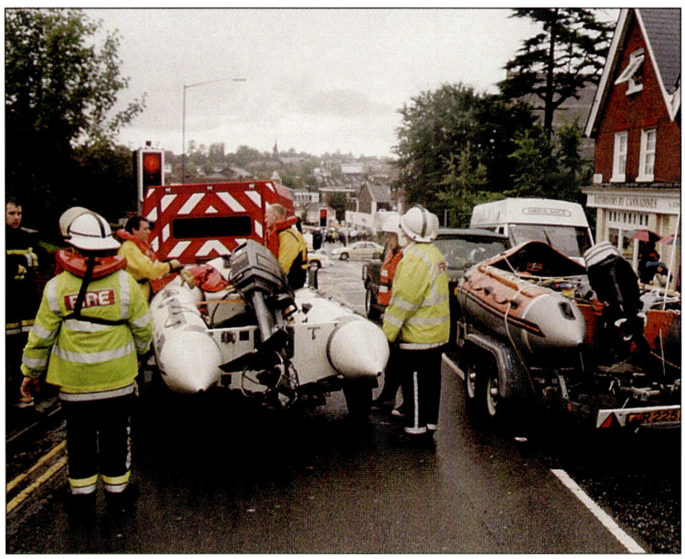

Lifeboats arrive in Uckfield to help with the rescues. Fire crews joined forces with the RNLI to offer help to people stranded after the deluge on the 12th October 2000. Picture John Elms.

The RNLI sent in crews from Eastbourne, Shoreham, Brighton and Hastings to help with the rescues after a desperate plea from Uckfield's fire crews. One RNLI crew got into difficulty and had to escape their uncontrollable craft by hanging onto railings. The town's fire station was under two feet of water and one crew transferred to a raft. The station was temporarily re-housed in the civic centre. Twenty people were rescued from the upper floor of Somerflelds. They included the nightshift employees. The rescued were checked and offered food and drinks at one of two rest centres set up by Wealden District Council at a local school. Incredibly, no-one was injured.

Two men on their way to work raced to the assistance of an elderly woman who started to disappear down a drain near the industrial estate. Ian Shears, 25, and Bill Chapman, 23, plucked the woman to safety at 6:15am. Firemen from Heathfleld helped ambulance men rescue an elderly lady from the second floor of Millington Court retirement home in Mill Lane.

The man swept away by the furious torrents was Vernon Bishop. The 58-year-old had gone to check his jewelry shop for flood damage shortly after 7am when he was bowled over by a "tidal wave". He was convinced he was going to die and only survived by clinging on to driftwood as the torrent carried him downstream until a coastguard helicopter crew spotted Mr Bishop half a mile away and winched him to safety.

The incident occurred just after he had unlocked the front door of the shop and was knocked over by a torrent flowing out from inside the shop. He was carried away by the strong currents rushing down the main street. Later, recovering in the Princess Royal Hospital, Haywards Heath, he told nurses:

"It was the most terrifying moment of my life. I thought I was going to die. The water came out of the shop like a huge wave crashing on to a beach. It picked me up and washed me away. I tried to grab hold of things but the water was moving so strongly. It pushed me down the High Street and into the river. I shouted at people to help but there was nothing they could do."

Hundreds of people got an unexpected day off work as a result of the chaos.

The previous night, Uckfield Community College had just brought the curtain down on its production of Noah and his Floating Zoo.

The rising waters turned the High Street into a tributary of the Uck. Tara Bean, landlady of the Cock and Bull public house in the High Street, came downstairs to find the pool table afloat in the main bar and £2,000 worth of stock ruined.The pub had recently been redecorated.

In the centre of town, cars once parked in neat displays on a garage forecourt lay scattered close to the railway station. A garden shed from several miles away floated down-river coming to rest on the roof of a Rover 216. The general manager of Caffyns Rover Garage in Uckfield found 12 of his cars damaged beyond repair. At least two had floated towards the town's main railway line, which was also closed.

The town was virtually split in two by the inundation. The Utopia Leisure Centre and the Ridgewood Resource Centre were converted into temporary shelters for those suffering from the effects of the floods. Buses were laid on to ferry evacuees to shelter.

In the weeks that followed, the townsfolk counted the cost of the most devastating floods they had ever witnessed.

A DAY TO REMEMBER IN LEWES

by Mark Davison

IT WAS a sleepless night in Lewes, the county town of East Sussex, on Wednesday October 11th 2000. Thunder woke people from their slumbers and stair-rod rain lashed at windows and rattled on roofs with an increasing roar. And just as one downpour ended, another started and seemed to be even more intense. So when news of Uckfield's invasion of water from the overflowing River Uck was broadcast on the radio at breakfast time it was not exactly a surprise to the tired and weary people getting up to go to school and work.

Plumpton, just to the north west of the historic town, turned out to be the wettest place in Britain. It collected an astonishing 144.5mm [5.66ins] of rain in the 24 hours up to 5pm that day. Few storms in the whole of the country had ever measured such a quantity. The storms had drifted inland from a warm sea and had been aggravated by the South Downs nearby. Lewes, at the foot of the hills, was the victim of the fallout.

Hundreds of homes, shops and offices were flooded to a depth of several feet in what turned out to be a major catastrophe.

Residents in Spences Lane, South Malling, were just some of the many people who were evacuated.

One man told of the dramatic events of that day on BBC's Southern Counties Radio. He said that he called at his girlfriend's house at dinner time on Thursday and "it was OK".

Not long after, the water came in through the front door and they had to put their tables on bricks. "By 3.30pm we were up to our waists downstairs and at 5pm my girlfriend realised that she'd left the front door keys downstairs," .He said I had to go down and get them and it was up to my neck by then. It was really, really cold. Around here, they got all the old people out and left us a bit, but eventually the RNLI came and took us out of the bedroom window. The water was within two steps from the top of the stairs. We had been trying to get everything upstairs. The crockery had been smashing as it floated along. We watched sheds floating down the road. Five or six cars disappeared under the water along the road.

'When we were rescued, the water was so high, we could just climb out of the upstairs windows and straight into the boat!

"Earlier, we had taken all the books and put them on top of the three-piece suite, thinking it would not come up, but then we were putting them on the stairs. But then it was coming up the stairs. I could not open the front door because of the force of the water. In the end we were in the pitch black. There was no power. We saw some people swimming about and an ambulance abandoned in the floods. I just wanted to get out of the house and get to dry land and have a cup of tea!

During the afternoon, the Phoenix Centre in town was a car park full of vehicles. By early evening it had totally disappeared with many of the cars submerged. The RNLI's regional headquarters were flooded out, too.

The town's Safeway store and car park were under at least four feet of water and by late evening, the sea of water near the bus station was giving out an ominous smell of diesel. Many of the shoppers' cars were barely visible. Those that were had water in them up to the steering wheel and door locks.

Late evening in Lewes, 12th October 2000 and shoppers' cars were trapped in Safeways Car Park as flood water from the river Ouse was held back by the incoming tide.

The Mayor, councillor Jim Daly and his team from the Lewes Royal Voluntary Service on hand helping the beleaguered flood victims evacuated to Lewes Town Hall.

Television crews were gathering in the centre and police were taping off the low-lying parts of the town. Flashing blue lights from the emergency vehicles reflected in the floodwaters, Above, a full moon was partly screened by ominous thunder clouds. Far off, over the sea, there were occasional flashes of lightning, as if the storm had moved aside to let the rescuers reach the mayhem.

Wading through the fast flowing river in search of the evacuation centre set up at Lewes Town Hall were Rupert Morley, 17, and Paul Davey, 18. "It's incredibly surreal," one of them said.

The muddy, waist-high torrents surged past Boots, WH Smith's and other chain stores as crowds watched from behind the police's blue and white tapes. Every so often, a fire engine or council vehicle ploughed through the floods creating bow waves and the waters crept up still further.

The Cliffe High Street was totally claimed by the new course of the River Ouse and The Fells area quickly went under. Large areas of Cliffe and South Malling were out of bounds and a huge evacuation programme was put into action.

Damage estimated at several million pounds was expected to result from the devastation.

In the freshly-painted Lewes Town Hall, the mayor, Councillor Jim Daly, of Lewes Town Council and members of the Lewes Royal Voluntary Service issued silver foil blankets and served tea and cakes to the beleagured people removed from their homes. A hamster and budgie arrived in their cages along with their owners. An elderly lady was tended to by paramedics. A young man in no fit mood to chat, sat with his head bowed between his knees, refusing to look up and talk. In the adjoining hall, children strewed toys all over the floor and seemed excited by the unexpected adventure.

By late evening on Thursday 12th October the lower half of Lewes High Street was a no go area for motorised transport except for the largest of council vehicles.

WRVS leader Sophie Anderson and her teams worked through the night. A table full of volunteers took names and addresses as the rescued arrived. Jeanette Allen, Conservative agent, arrived, somehow, from Brighton to offer comforting words to the traumatised. "The neighbourliness has been tremendous," she said in her strong Scottish accent. "Some are shell shocked. There are families here, women, children and dogs. They suddenly had a large ornamental lake spread out in front of them. They were incredulous."

Council workers, the Red Cross and WRVS also ran another rest centre at the Malling Community Centre. Showers were made available at the Lewes Leisure Centre.

In the lowest parts of the town, the water was six feet deep. All buses and trains into Lewes were cancelled. More than 100 homes were evacuated in the South Street, Timberyard Lane and Morris Road area as well as the lower reaches of Landport. One house in Orchard Road had water up to within six inches of the ceiing. Valerie Richardson cried, saying she was "very depressed and absolutely gutted".

An internal wall at Harvey's Brewery collapsed, beer barrels floated away and four men were seen trapped on a roof. Cattle were rounded up at Landport and temporarily herded into the grounds of a primary school.

Villages near Lewes were also badly hit. Barcombe Mills was blocked and Plumpton was impassable from the south. The cellar of the Royal Oak public house in Barcombe was flooded with five feet of water and people in properties along the banks of the Ouse were evacuated from their homes.

Royal Mail planned to destroy 70,000 letters and packages contaminated with effluent because of the potential healthrisk. The sorting and delivery office had to be transferred to Brighton.

Some 2,500 premises in Lewes were without power after a substation had floodwater rising all around it. Seeboard decided to sever supplies before it caused an even greater disruption. The water had reached within six inches of the sub-station by 11pm. Southern Counties radio warned people: Look out now, before midnight, for torches and candles. If you have a flask, fill it up with hot water If you have a baby, heat milk now and put it in a flask. Get batteries in for your radio."

Mike James, from Seeboard, made an urgent appeal for people not to bake cakes or use their washing machines. Power supplies had to be conserved.

But people were far too busy to bake cakes. They were climbing into lifeboats and fleeing their homes. A high tide was expected at 1:30am and it delayed the draining away of huge volumes of floodwater. Pippa Gordon, Southern Counties presenter said: "It's all so bewildering."

One listener rang from a flat high above the torrents. He said on air: "What's distressing is watching children's toys being washed away. A paddling pool has just floated past. It's absolutely devastating!"

A man broke his leg during the night's dramatic activities, but remarkably there appeared to be no other injuries treated by paramedics.

The fire brigade had to evacuate its own control room after water poured in. At the Volunteer Inn, customers formed a chain to get stock out of the cellar onto the darkened bars. There was trouble lifting the heavy fruit machine. At the back of the pub, a Sierra car was engulfed in five feet of floodwater.

The world's media swamped the BBC's switchboard. How do you spell Lewes? How do you pronounce it?"

Children had an unexpected holiday when the town's schools shut.

Drowned cattle could be seen in the fields at Malling. A dead horse was found in the Southover area. More than 50 British Red Cross volunteers were drafted in to help flood victims.

Lewes railway line was submerged under three feet of water. Looters from Tunbridge Wells, Brighton, Hastings and Eastbourne ransacked homes and shops while the owners were away. St John Castro Church was also raided. Three men were found ransacking Safeway for cigarettes and alcohol. Six arrests were made.

A 15-year-old boy escaped from a first floor window as water engulfed his home in Spences Lane. In a rucksack, he had placed his pet cat.

Flood hero Andrew Grassie was staying at his mother-in-law's in Morris Road when the River Ouse sent torrents of water through the Cliffe area. Andrew, his wife Sara, and her mother were in a first floor room of the house at 3pm watching the waters rise. From the house opposite, they heard shouting and saw a young woman desperately waving at them. Andrew climbed from the window and part waded, part swam to the house opposite to investigate. He discovered that an elderly Italian woman was struggling to keep her head above the water in her kitchen. She had been trapped by a toppled freezer. "She was hanging onto it for dear life and failing," he told the Sussex Express.

Fortunately extra help was on the way. Moments later, a paramedic and doctor arrived and the lady was rescued.

There was a dreamlike mood in Lewes on Thursday evening, a surreal world of dancing lights as the waters rose ever higher.

THE FLOODS CONTINUE...

Above: East Farleigh's narrow bridge held firm against the might of the swollen river Medway. Picture by Pat Ollive.

On Saturday 28th October a cold front swept east across southern districts accompanied by heavy rain a tornado formed in Bognor Regis, West Sussex. In classic style it tore a narrow path of damage one and half miles long through Bognor Regis, West Sussex. Within this corridor over 100 houses suffered broken windows, fallen chimneys, smashed greenhouses and damaged roofs. Five people were injured; including two women at Riverside Caravan Park when a caravan was lifted clean into the air and dropped onto another parked nearby. 140 fire fighters were involved in the emergency.

Now an even worse foe was to strike. The worst storm since January 1990 was gathering strength in the Atlantic. On Sunday afternoon 29th rain set in from the south-west, as a deep low lay close to western Scotland. The wind became very strong blowing at severe gale force 9 with gusts to 100 mph at The Needles. A person died and two were injured as an oak tree toppled onto a car at Hindhead. During the early hours as an intense secondary low moved north east across Wales to north east England wind gusts inland touched 70 mph. Mayhem resulted. The saturated soils loosened roots and hundreds of trees toppled. Very heavy rain resulted in widespread flooding, many places receiving 50mm [2 inches], nearly a month's rain. In northern England as the low moved across at breakfast time heavy rain turned to snow ,15cm [6 inches] deep near Durham shutting the A66 and closing the Snake Pass in Derbyshire. The morning rush hour was almost brought to a halt further south. The police advised commuters not to travel and many people heeded the advice. There were 41 severe flood warnings. Three ferries with several thousand passengers were stranded off Dover and rode out the mountainous seas offshore unable to make it through the harbour entrance. The port was closed to all shipping. A train hit a fallen tree on the Heathrow line bringing services to a halt and elsewhere many trains were cancelled as an estimated 1000 trees toppled across tracks. A landslide blocked the Glasgow to Edinburgh line and another shut the London–Brighton line at Hassocks. 100 flights were cancelled from London's Airports and even the London Eye was halted as the force of the wind broke the glass from six of its capsules.

Homes were evacuated from Cornwall to Kent as floods engulfed floodplains. At Gunnislake near Taunton one man was winched to safety from his submerged house by helicopter as the River Tamar burst its banks.

Another tornado was reported on the south coast hitting Selsey, not far from Bognor. Winds were estimated at 90 mph, and more caravans were damaged. The air pressure fell to 944 millibars [27.88 inches] as the storm passed into the North Sea. This was lower than measured during the October 1987 and January 1990 great gales and was the lowest on record for October.

The M25 became a vast empty lake near junction 9. Only the sound of lapping water and rustling of leaves on adjacent trees could be heard at a time when normally 50,000 vehicles an hour would be thundering past. The busy A3 too was a ghostly hush as Bolder Mere Lake engulfed the highway close to the intersection with the M25 at junction 10.

Across the country over 100,000 homes were without electricity but for residents of Robertsbridge in Sussex and Lamberhurst in Kent the sickening sight of surging flood water overtopping the banks of the normally tranquil Rother and Teise streams was too much to bear. Posters advertising previous flood appeals lay floating in the waters. They were still clearing up from the devastation earlier in the month when some residents had faced bills of up to £30,000 to repair their homes and businesses.

There were several more deaths; a motor cyclist hit a tree near Taunton and a van was blown into the path of a truck in Lincolnshire killing its driver. Flood water caused a car to go out of control in London and the driver died when it hit a bus.

The month ended with sunny spells and a dry day but people were being evacuated from the Medway Valley in the Yalding area as the combined waters of the Rivers Beult, Medway and Teise swamped the area. Five 100 tonne barges were threatening to break loose from their moorings near Allington Maidstone and bear down on the lock. The heavy rain had loosened concrete blocks to which they were attached. Steel cables were finally fastened to the barges and secured.

Would the weather relent, the rain clouds roll back and high pressure take charge? The answer was given in dramatic style. One of the deepest lows to cross southern England in November gave another deluge on Guy Fawkes Night.

There was relief for people who had planned their bonfire party for Saturday 4th, as the evening was fine and crisp. But some venues were too water logged. At Leeds Castle in Kent, a Grand Firework Spectacular had to be cancelled.

Left: Villages along the Medway valley suffered badly with Yalding severely hit. Here at East Farleigh the floods were an exciting adventure for the young. Picture by Simon Haswell

After several weeks of the river Medway running high a deluge in December was the last straw for these vessels at Wateringbury, Kent, December 12th 2000.

CASELLA

The Environmental Company

200 Years of Meteorology

Classical meteorological instrumentation has been a key part of the Casella range since the very beginning. In the Great Exhibition of 1862 we won the only bronze medal for registering meteorological instruments and throughout the 19th and 20th centuries we have maintained our commitment to supplying classical met. equipment in enthusiasts and professionals alike, with products like copper rain gauges, the Campbell Stokes Sunshine recorder and tradtional Stevenson Screens.

METEOROLOGY LOOKING FORWARD

Whilst very proud with our heritage in the meteorological world, we must also maintain our commitment to new technologies. In recent years, this development has given us the NEMESYS; an off-the-shelf weather monitoring package, the MULTI-MET; a professional, yet affordable wind speed and direction system and our latest creation; the Heated Tipping Bucket Rain Gauge; the solution for rainfall measuring in extreme climates.

NEW PRODUCT LAUNCH

The well established and popular Tipping Bucket Rain Gauge has been further enhancedto enclude a heating facility for customers who require accurate and reiable rain under extreme weather conditions.

Its versatility allows it to incorporated into a simple rainfall logging, or fully automated meteorological of hydrological monitoring system.

Manufactured to the high structural benefits of its predecessor, e.g. case aluminium alloy base and built-in spirit level. The heater element itself is operated via an adjustable thermostat, which is factory-set to switch the heater on at 3°C. This will ensure that the mechanism is always kept above freezing.

Features

- 0.1, 0.2 or 0.5 mm bucket sizes available
- Operating temperatuer range of -20 to +85°C
- Highly accurate, precision-made gauge (±1% @ 1litre/hour)
- Logging system available for independent data collection

Applications

- Measurement of solid and liquid precipitation
- Rainfall measurement in extreme climates
- Hydrological modelling of specific catchment areas using a rain gauge network

Regent House, Wolsely Road, Kempston, Bedford MK42 7JY
Tel: 01234 844100 Fax: 01234 841490
e-mail: info@casella.co.uk web: www.casella.co.uk

THE SUREST MEASURE OF A CHANGING WORLD

The flooding in York was the worst back to at least the 1600s. The river Ouse came to with a few centimetres of the city's flood defences peaking at 5.4metres[17.7feet] but even so 5,000 properties suffered damage. Over 70,000 sandbags were deployed and hunderds of police, army and council personnel fought a long hard battle to avoid an even greater disaster.
All pictures of York taken by Alex Watson of York Vision, Website Address, www.yorkvision.co.uk

York was in a serious position as the large Ouse catchment area was outpouring weeks of accumulated rain. By Monday, morning of the 6th over 70,000 sandbags had been deployed in the city using 1000 tonnes of sand. 500 army, police and fire personnel helped in evacuating people from the most threatened areas of the city.

A record 52 severe flood warnings were issued as another 50mm [2 inches] of rain fell in many places. Government ministers visited key areas on fact-finding missions. John Prescott donned Environment Agency waders and stood up to his waist in murky swirling waters in Norton, north Yorkshire close to the river Derwent.

People had only just recovered from floods last year. The Prime Minister, Tony Blair, clad in raincoat and 'wellies', visited Bewdley and Shrewsbury on the Severn. Insurance expects were quoting estimated damage of £400 million pounds nation-wide.

The Ouse at York peaked at 5.4m [17.7 feet], just 5cm below the height of the city's main flood defences but even so 5,000 properties were affected and it was deemed the worst inundation since the 1600s.

There were similar scenes along the river Severn where it reached its highest level since March 1947 at 4.5 metres [14.7 feet] with Worcester and Shrewsbury badly affected. Seventy orthopaedic patients were evacuated from the Royal Infirmary at Worcester.

Autumn rainfall totals beat long term records at Coulsdon, Surrey. Records for this area go back over a 100 years and by the 8th November the previous wettest autumn measured in 1974 of 413mm was exceeded.

November continued wet and by the end of the month this figure had increased to 506.8mm making it the wet-

test season on record, beating the winter of 1914/15 by 1.9mm.

This astonishing total represents around 5,000 tonnes of water on an area the size of a football pitch. This produced an exceptional rise of groundwater levels.

It was even wetter in Sussex and springs, which had been dormant for centuries, were coming back to life. At Patcham in Sussex the A23 was shut for several weeks as streams poured through houses and across the road. Chichester became festooned with 70 miles of pipeline in an operation to save The Hornet. The river Lavant swollen by springs was flowing at 6.1 cubic metres per second. The word `lavant' means intermittent stream.

November ended with up to 25mm of rain and further flooding with the A22 shut at Halland in Sussex. With the land so saturated any further storms would prove disastrous and winter lay ahead.

Some of York's 70,000 sandbags used to stem the flooding.

In Worcester the floods came to within a foot of the 1947Great Flood. The main bridge was twice closed across the river Severn and the Territorial Army used their trucks to link the two severed parts of the city. This picture shows Hylton Road under water. Picture by Edward Webley

View across the flooded playing fields adjacent to Worcester Cricket Ground with the cathedral in the background. Picture by Edward Webley

At Leith Hill, SE England's highest point, a landslip carried away the road. It looked like the aftermath of a tremendous earthquake. Huge Cedar trees toppled as the ground over a wide area slipped four feet creating huge cracks and fissures.

This article was reported by a local newspaper during the tremendous weather conditions in Hampshire. A surprise catch indeed!

Flooding led to a surprise catch for a fishing shop owner when he picked up a 10lb salmon swimming up the high street in Ringwood, Hampshire.

Andy Browne cornered the salmon in a car park, scooped it up and returned it to the river Avon, which has overflowed, with the recent weather conditions.

A peaceful scene here at Datchet near Windsor but the river Thames was running high on 9th November 2000 and not a place to sit down and enjoy the view.

There is no doubt that autumn 2000 has seen some record-breaking weather. It has been a lively talking point in the office, the pub, the high street and in The Hague where the end of the World Conference on limiting Global warming was as stormy as the Weather itself.

Some extraordinary rainfall totals were measured in many parts of Britain especially the Southeast and North east of England, areas which are often the driest part of the British Isles. Places in Sussex for instance recorded more rain during the autumn than would normally fall during the entire year in London or Norwich. The air pressure was constantly low, making some people think their barometers had broken. November's average air pressure was the lowest of any month on record. During September, October and the whole of November there were no dry spells at all. By the end of the autumn, so much rain had fallen on the South and North Downs that it was bursting out at the spring line as `bournes', gushing forth millions of gallons of water. Such an event is very unusual in autumn for it normally takes until the end of the winter for water to percolate though the chalk. Over England and Wales, it has proved the wettest such period since rainfall figures have been collated from 1766.

Local Farmer Rodney Fuller takes his dogs to look at the stream flow in the Halliloo Valley near Caterham on the 29th November 2000. It is known locally as The Bourne, and is an intermittent stream, one of hundreds which have risen as a result of the prolonged heavy autumnal rains. It is very unusual to flow in the autumn as it takes some time for water to percolate through the chalk downs.

This 'Flood Special' issue was held up by the floods. The printers, Litho Techniques, are being approached here by boat on December 16th 2000 as the River Bourne started to flood in a normally dry valley. Over 600mm [24inches] of rain or the equivalent of London's annual rainfall,was measured in under 3 months, causing a dramatic rise of the water table.

This book is recommended by the Editor.

Top: 13 miles of pipeline were used in the centre of Chichester to prevent the river Lavant from flooding The Hornet, Westhampnett and St. Pancras areas of the city. The pipes can carry 50 tonnes of water a minute. Businesses in Chichester prepared to face the floods if the huge pumping operation failed. In 1994 the Lavant burst its banks in the worst floods since1852 after drying up completely in 1992. Below: The Chichester Observers severe weather headlines. Bottom right: A sign in the window of a Guildford business flooded by the river Wey. Pictures by Mark Davison.

...AND THE FLOODS GO ON

December continued very unsettled with one Atlantic weather system after another sweeping across the country. 200 people had to be airlifted from a caravan park at Dawlish Warren in Devon after 40mm of rain caused flash floods and at Credition two people were killed when it was thought that a driver took the wrong turn on a flooded road and drove into a swollen river. At the end of the first week there were140 Flood Watches in operation issued by the Environment Agency.

On the evening of the 12th, the wind reached 93mph at Mumbles in South Wales and many places recorded 20-25 mm of rain. The Environment Agency issued this message which graphically illustrated the serious situation.

" ***The Agency is receiving reports almost on an hourly basis from across the South of homes being flooded that have never been flooded before. In the current unprecedented conditions where the ground is super saturated all homes and businesses in the floodplain must consider themselves to be at potential risk from serious flooding and should take as many precautions as possible. Even homes which are outside the flood plain are being flooded due to field and road runoff and ground water problems.***"

On the morning of the 13th December after an intense low pressure system had moved north east over the Irish Sea there were 18 severe flood warnings and 100 lesser ones. At Shrewsbury the river Severn was running at 4.7 metres, nearly 5 times the average level flooding properties for the third time in as many months. Overnight the M23 in Sussex had closed south of Crawley due to floodwater at junction 10.

Residents were moved from a block of flats in Cardiff when the roof was blown off, again passengers faced a terrible night on ferries prevented from entering Dover, and the port of Felixstowe was shut. The M1 was shut at junction 17 as lorries were blown over and south of Peterborough and in the Hitchin area fallen power cables closed railway lines. 70,000 homes and businesses suffered power cuts in East Anglia.

FLOODS, TEMPESTS AND FUTURE WEATHER IS OUR CLIMATE CHANGING?

Ian Currie

AUTUMN 2000 is not the only occasion we have experienced severe weather. In AD 48 10,000 persons were reported to have drowned along the Thames and much property destroyed. In AD 353, a great flood took place in Cheshire, 5,000 persons and an innumerable quantity of cattle perished. Similarly, in 1099 on November 11th, a violent storm at high tide flooded the coasts of Holland and England as far south as Kent with thousands of deaths. Winchelsea on the Sussex coast suffered badly with 300 houses and a number of churches destroyed on 1st October 1250.

One of the worst floods took place in 1282 when a terrific gale brought great suffering to Lincolnshire especially Boston and in East Anglia. Contemporary accounts stated that "In Yarmouth, Donwich and Ipchurch an intolerable multitude of men, women and children were overwhelmed by the waters."

There is much evidence to suggest that an exceptionally severe gale in 1362 was more powerful than the October 1987 storm. On the 23rd January [New Style] a tempest blew down bell towers at Bury St Edmunds, Norwich and London. It affected the southern half of Britain whilst another potent storm in 1421 produced a great surge and the resultant flood broke over Friesland, Holland and England. Some 72 towns were submerged and 100,000 people drowned. Another fearful storm took place in April 1446 and thousands died around the shores of the North Sea.

The period from the eleventh to the fifteenth centuries was exceptionally stormy in areas bordering the North Sea.

In 1607 on January 20th, a disastrous flood occurred around the Severn Estuary. Stow records that "the waters rose above the tops of the houses. It was due to an unusually high spring tide encountering an exceptional run-off in the Severn. Also the Fens in the east were badly flooded and at Broom Hill in Romney Marsh "the sea came in so outrageously that one Master Bury lost 1,162 sheep and the area looked beyond reclamation" whilst in 1662 the on the 28th January [New Style] a storm blew with such force as to cause severe damage to buildings and a vast number of trees were felled". It seems the worst effects were felt across the south Midlands.

A storm that was arguably greater in magnitude than anything since struck places south of Birmingham after midnight on 26th November 1703 with tragic consequences. The death toll amounting to 8,000 to possibly 15,000 people, many lost at sea. The Reverend Derham wrote "the Sea raging in such a manner that in some parts of England 'twas incredible, the Water rising six or seven feet higher than was ever known to do in the Memory of Man". It was reported that "above 80 people" were drowned in the surge along the Severn estuary. Daniel Defoe living in London at the time said," I could barely believe a hundredth part of what I saw".

Sand a metre deep or more was deposited in coastal areas of Lincolnshire on the night of the 31st January 1953. A number of people were drowned and in places such as Sutton-on –Sea and Mablethorpe in Lincolnshire the sea swept several miles inland. Picture courtesy of Robin Stirling.

The east coast took a pounding in 1978 when on the 11th January the wind reached 80 mph and huge seas destroyed piers at Harwich and Margate and damaged the railway line here at Mablethorpe, Lincolnshire. Picture by Robin Stirling.

A similar storm affected the northern half of Britain on the 7th January 1839. It was responsible for the deaths of at least 139 people. Thousands of trees were blown down, hundreds of buildings destroyed and many ships were wrecked. Another January tempest wrought terrible havoc in 1881. Between the 18th and 21st January a severe snow laden easterly gale brought tremendous disruption to the southern half of Britain with an accompanying high tide producing floods along the Thames and the East Coast. One hundred barges were sunk on the Thames alone with £2 million worth of damage to property.

The death toll in this blizzard was estimated to have reached over 100 throughout southern England.

In March 1947 after several weeks of prolonged cold and snow which had accumulated to level depths of two metres in Teesdale and Denbighshire milder air made its way across England by the 11th and a rapid thaw ensued. The combination of still frozen ground, heavy rain and melt waters led to huge areas of Britain turned into vast lakes; the Severn, Wye, Thames, Medway and Trent all burst their banks as did the Fenland rivers such as the Ouse. Winds gusted to 100mph adding to the chaos. The whole lower Trent Valley was flooded with 70 per cent of Selby's houses inundated.

A disaster that matched anything before it took place in 1953 on January 31st-February 1st. A deep depression moved south-east to just west of Denmark and the attendant steep pressure gradient caused a violent northerly gale in the North Sea. This led to a storm surge, which enhanced tide levels. At King's Lynn the tide was 2.5 metres higher than predicted. Some 150,000 million cubic metres of water were forced from the Atlantic to the North Sea. The net result was sea and river defences were breached or overtopped in a number of places, and widespread flooding took place between the Tees and Dover. The death toll exceeded 300 in Britain with 119 people in Essex losing their lives. The tragedy in Holland was even greater with casualties here and elsewhere along the North Sea coast reaching several thousand. The disaster could have been even worse if the spring tide had been above average and if the level of the Thames and its tributaries had been raised by heavy rainfall or melting snow as they were in January 1928. It is almost certain that London would not have escaped.

The second half of the twentieth century brought an increasing number of storms with 1968 an extreme example. On the 15th January, a severe gale in the Glasgow area enhanced by the convergence of the wind through the Clyde-Forth gap caused damage to 340,000 buildings and the total repair costs exceeded £30million. High-tension cables across the Clyde were blown down bringing a suspension to shipping. In the North Sea the oil-rig Sea Quest snapped her anchor. On Great Dun Fell in the northern Pennines the wind speed reached 133mph. Over 600 troops were needed to assist with rehabilitation work and 856 people needed rehousing. The most distressing fact was that 20 people were killed and 38 injured.

This year also saw three major rainstorms. The first took place on 26-27th March in the Scottish Highlands in a relatively unpopulated area but those of the 11th July and 14-15th September affected many parts of England including the densely populated Southeast. In July 14,000 sq. miles had over 50mm [2 inches] of rain flooding farmland from Devon to Lincolnshire. As many as a thousand bridges were brought down.

In September, parts of the Southeast had as much as 200mm [8 inches] of rain in just 48 hours, one third of the annual total. Thousands of homes were flooded with Molesey in Surrey and Edenbridge in Kent among some of the worst affected places. Many bridges were washed away including the A281 Horsham-Guildford road bridge at Shalford. The total cost amounted to £6 million. Unusual amounts of sea ice off Iceland and Greenland may have triggered these events.

In 1976 made famous by its hot dry summer, the year began with a deep area of low pressure moving across Scotland into the North Sea causing winds to the south of its track to reach hurricane force. Gusts exceeded 105mph at Wittering and 102mph in Norwich with a gust of 134mph at Lowther Hill, Strathclyde. Structural damage was widespread in virtually every county but the most severe damage was felt in a band across Northern Ireland, Lancashire and the Midlands to East Anglia. Fallen trees blocked every road out of Norwich. Damage was put at £100 million over the country as a whole.

In January 1978 a "wave" depression rapidly deepened into an intense storm which crossed the Midlands and East Anglia. In its wake a severe northerly gale whipped up a tidal surge almost as bad as 1953. Winds gusted to over 80mph destroying piers at Margate and Harwich. The flooding of coastal property caused £5 million of damage to Kent alone. The city of London narrowly escaped disaster as the water came to within 19 inches of the top of the retaining walls. The Thames Flood Barrier was started this year with the lessons of this storm reinforcing the need to complete it.

Still vivid in many southerners' minds is October 1987. On the 16th, a storm almost comparable to the 1703 event caused some three million households to be without electricity. In a few manic hours 15 million trees were felled and one in six households filed an insurance claim with the overall cost at £2.5 thousand million pounds. The cause was a rapidly deepening area of low pressure that moved north-east from Devon to the Wash.

In 1990, the 25th January produced another epic storm as a low `explosively deepened' out in the Atlantic and moved eastward across southern Scotland. With the storm reaching its peak during the day the death toll was greater than 1987, 47 fatalities compared to 18 in the former. It also affected more of the country and was followed by several more storms during February. There was serious flooding along the Severn, Thames and Wye Valleys as well as the Kent, Sussex and Lancashire coasts.

The worst was reserved for the North Wales coast at Towyn. Another three million

The Chelsea Reservoir at Walton On Thames, Surrey in August 1976 during the drought. Picture from the Surrey Weather Book.

trees were felled, hundreds of thousands of homes were without electricity and the insurance cost was put at over £2 thousand million.

During this time 1987-1992 a drought affected the South and East of Britain and was the most serious and prolonged since 1740. The rainfall deficit amounted to around 460mm in places or some 75 per cent of the annual rainfall in the drier parts. Among the problems caused by the lack of rainfall was subsidence due to shrinkage of clay.

These events are by no means an exhaustive list of storms that have pounded our shores and countryside. But they are enough to demonstrate that whilst the British climate is thought of as being equable it is subject to a variety of climatic hazards which have exacted a high toll in both life and property throughout history. Research shows that in pre-Norman Conquest times the weather was generally warmer and more settled than today. In the Middle Ages the weather deteriorated into what is termed the "Little Ice Age" with average temperatures dropping by several degrees leading to some harsh winters and increased storminess.

A slow warming has been indicated since 1900 with a greater acceleration since 1970. Remember 1976. This summer saw the culmination of a severe drought that had its roots back to May 1975. In a sixteen months spell rainfall averaged out in places to just 40 per cent. The summer of 1976 saw 14 consecutive days with the mercury above 32C [90F] somewhere in southern England. Water was rationed, crops failed, grass withered and milk yields depleted. Farm expenditure rose by 20 per cent, fire fighting costs in tinder dry woodland amounted to £2.5 million. Thousands of buildings were affected by ground subsidence due to the desiccation of clay soils. Insurance claims totalled £60 million. Since then records for warmth have tumbled with August 3rd 1990 reaching 37.2C [99F] at Cheltenham. The months of November 1994, August 1995, and October 1995 all have exceeded previous values, as did the very mild winter of 1990. Evidence suggests that the decade 1990-1999 has been the warmest of the past millennium ***(See issue 4 page 5).***

Future weather....? by Peter Zebedee

Certainly, it could be argued that extreme weather has become more frequent in the latter half of the twentieth century. This may be in response to the increased warming globally as this would heighten the thermal gradient between the cold Greenland ice cap and the warmer Atlantic waters leading to increasing energy in Atlantic storm systems.

Because most winters during the 1990s have been mild subtropical and Mediterranean plant species have been thriving at The Royal Horticultural Society Gardens at Rosemoor, north Devon.

SOME REMARKABLE OCTOBER 2000 RAINFALL TOTALS IN MM			
Place	**County**	**Amount mm**	**% of long term average**
Plumpton	East Sussex	343	318
Barcombe	East Sussex	339	364
Hurstpierpoint	West Sussex	331	
Mayfield	Kent	317	
Iping Mill	West Sussex	257	347
Chartham	Kent	256	350
Ardingly	East Sussex	253	287
South Reigate	Surrey	230	
Storrington	West Sussex	222	
Warlingham	Surrey	213	
Coulsdon	Surrey	203	212

One of the main reasons for the Floods of 2000 has been warmer than average ocean temperatures to the south of the Azores combined with cooler seas to the north west of Britain. This has strengthened the jet stream, a narrow current of fast moving air that can be thousands of miles long. It can often travel at a velocity of 100 mph or more at a height of around 35,000 feet. Its alignment normally steers low-pressure systems between Iceland and Scotland but during autumn 2000 its position has had the effect of encouraging them to form and move in more southerly latitudes towards Britain.

The impact of a terrible storm is made worse when a number of hazards act together. For instance heavy snowfalls may be replaced by a rapid thaw as an intense depression crosses Britain into the North Sea. If this happens at a time of high spring tides and high river levels, a southward moving tidal storm surge initiated by the storm would cause a great deal of damage along the east coast. Devastation inland would be widespread if gusts rose to over 80mph, the threshold for extensive damage. Such events have occurred though not necessarily meeting all these criteria, for example 1928, 1947 and 1953. The latter though causing great loss of life could have been even more serious if the winter had not been dry and Spring tides were not exceptionally high. With a gradual geological downwarping of Southeast Britain coupled with a possible rise of sea level induced by expansion of the sea as global temperatures increase and polar land ice melts low-lying coastal areas would seem to be at particular risk from flooding during the 21st century.

Climate changes over the past 2,000 years have lasted several hundred years and at the beginning and end of such events, there is evidence of increased storminess.

Temperatures changed by several degrees C over these periods. The present evidence for warming comes at a time when anthropomorphic influences such as the churning out of vast amounts of carbon dioxide and methane into the atmosphere, 'The Greenhouse Effect', is overriding natural change for the first time in Man's history. Temperatures could increase at a rate that our flora and fauna will find difficulty in adapting to. A degree change in a 100 years may now be realised in just 25 and 4C in a century is one mighty modification to the climate. More frequent summer droughts and heavier autumnal and winter rains are to be expected though still with the chance of one or two cold winters as happened in AD 1092 near the peak of the Medieval Warm Period.

Perhaps keep that toboggan a while longer but plant a vine as well

The summer of 1990, like 1989, was a great year for grapes, and vintage wine was plentiful at Headley Farm near Leatherhead, and on the slopes above Dorking. Pictured above Guy Woodall of Leatherhead's Thorncroft Vineyard showing the bumper crop in 1990. Picture from the Surrey Weather Book.

Tune into Telewest's Cable 17 Local News programme for South London and see Weather Eye Editor Ian Currie. He is pictured here (right) with Jon Dixon (Left). Apart from giving a comprehensive forecast he conducts Weather experiments, answers questions and shows off his notable collection of Weather jumpers.

A WORLD OF BAROMETERS

by Philip Collins(F.R. Met.S).

***"The barometer is one of the most valuable instruments ever contrived for investigating the nature and laws of the wonderful ocean of air in which we live"* Admiral Fitzroy.**

The barometer must be one of the most curious instruments made. Although it is built to measure air pressure it is consulted daily in almost ritual fashion to try and interpret the vagaries of our English weather. No other scientific instrument has entered into the home as a piece of furniture like the barometer.

I suppose I must confess to being a barometer-phile and as with most passions, the more one gets into the subject the more engrossed one becomes. Having been interested in antiques since before I left school I searched antique markets and jumble sales in the hunt for a bargain. After a few early career changes, from banking to computers, I moved from my Berkshire home at Maidenhead to live in Devon. After a while I started working for an antique restorer, restoring furniture and the cases of antique barometers when they came in.

For my 21st birthday my parents paid for an antique barometer and I restored it. Looking back, it was a sad wreck and the dealer must have been pleased to be shot of it! It was certainly a challenge.

Since then, having gone self employed, I repaired barometers increasingly, so much so that ten years ago we re-named our antique business to its current title *'Barometer world'* as we work in a "world of barometers".

It is quite astounding the variety of barometers that have been made over the centuries for various purposes and decoration. I was fortunate to be offered Edwin Banfield's Family Collection of barometers for display. They form the basis of our museum here at Merton in Devon with over 300 examples. I now collect a few as they come along to augment this incredible collection and we have expanded in this small village to employ five craftsmen restoring barometers and occasionally making fine copies.

Having written two books on barometers — Care and Restoration of Barometers and recently Aneroid Barometers and their Restoration — I am now beginning to work on my third barometer book.

Some of our more unusual barometers such as sympiesometers, a snorting barometer, the donkey barometer, Huygens barometers, Amontons barometers, mining barometer, altimeters as well as the usual pockets, sticks and wheels, will perhaps begin to show readers that there is a lot more behind the barometer than first meets the eye. I hope in future issues of *Weather Eye* to be able to explain some of their workings and interesting features that I have unearthed over the years including the use of wild oats in barometers! After all, the barometer is still the most important single instrument for predicting the weather.

Barometer World ■ Merton ■ Devon EX 20 3DS
Telephone: 01805 603 443 ■ Fax: 01805 603 334

ISBN 0-9534240-3-0